GET ATTITUDE !

PRAISE FOR GLENN BILL

"Glenn Bill is in the top .0002% of business leaders in North America today...you can trust that he stands ready to deliver excellence and exceed your expectations."

- **DARREN HARDY**, *New York Times*
Best Selling Author of *The Compound Effect*
and Publisher of *SUCCESS* Magazine

"Coach Bill's book has helped me thoroughly assess my attitude, as well as my ability to interact at a higher level with my peers. He has profoundly assisted me with great professional developmental tools. Great insights!"

- **DUJUAN DANIELS**, *Super Bowl Champion*
New England Patriots National Scout

"Engage with Glenn, he delivers high-energy with a side of humor, and he is passionate about it. My personal advice, don't just hire Glenn, get to know him and his story...great guy!"

- **JEFFREY GITOMER**, Hall of Fame Speaker,
Sales Trainer and *New York Times* Best Selling Author

"In all my years of football, I've never had a coach that got me more ready and mentally prepared to go into a game like Coach Bill."

- **ZACH MARTIN**, *All-Pro Offensive Lineman*, Dallas Cowboys

"Glenn's message lasted more than just a day for our organization. He was memorable, energetic, relevant to today's market, and he just 'gets' what most speakers don't!"

- **WARREN HARLING**, Branch Manager, President's Club Member, *MetLife Home Loans*

"Glenn has been a student of my training for over 20 years. His dedication to professionalism is admirable. He lives what works. I recommend that you give serious consideration to engaging him to create positive momentum for your company or team."

- **TOM HOPKINS**, Author of the National Best Seller *How to Master the Art of Selling*

"Glenn is unbelievable. It is rare to find an experienced business owner and salesperson who has walked the talk like Glenn. His presentation came from his heart and the road of hard knocks. We love Glenn's no nonsense, positive, direct, and enthusiastic presentation style. Every time he speaks to our 300 agent sales force, he lights their fire!"

- **MICK SCHEETZ**, Broker/Owner, *CENTURY 21 Scheetz*

"Glenn's message delivered real, tangible solutions my salespeople could implement right now! Great creativity, thoughts and ideas! He did an excellent job."

- **STEVE JACOBSON**, President,
Fairway Mortgage

"Glenn's enthusiasm, energy, and delivery is just what my company needed at our kickoff event. His ideas were original and his ability to get my agents to think differently was eye opening and motivational."

- **JAMES BRADLEY**, Broker/Owner,
CENTURY 21 Bradley

The ABCs of Attitude: Discover The Secret Formula to Achieve Success In Your Personal and Business Life, Increase Your Emotional Intelligence and GET ATTITUDE

University of Attitude

GB Unlimited, Inc.
4929 E. 96th
Indianapolis, IN 46240 USA

Phone: (317) 590-7757
Email: gbill@UniversityofAttitude.com

www.UniversityOfAttitude.com

Ordering Information

Special discounts are available on quantity purchases by corporations, associations, and other organizations. For details, contact the publisher at the address above.

Editing: Carly Carruthers
Composition and design: Barnum Media Group

Hardcover ISBN: 978-0-9963911-0-8

The author of this book does not dispense medical advice or perscribe the use of any technique as a form of treatment for physical, emotional, or medical problems without the advice of a physician, either directly or indirectly. The intent of the author is only to offer information of a general nature to help you in your quest for emotional and spiritual well-being. In the event you use any of the information in this book for yourself, the author and the publisher assume no responsibility for your actions.

Printed in the United States of America

I dedicate this book to my lovely wife Colleen and our children, Brittany, Anthony, Alex and Christopher.

I also dedicate this book to my parents (Joe and Gracie), siblings (Joe, Molly, Jude, and Brian) and my wife's family.

As well as all my extended family members, including those from theBishop Chatard Football Family and my CENTURY 21 Real Estate Family.

———◆———

Also a Thank You to:

Jason and his team at the Barnum Media Group and all the professional speakers and authors who inspired me.

CONTENTS

Part Three
Make a Difference
with Your New Attitude!

Part Four
The Attitude of Effort

PREFACE

People will pick up this book for many different reasons. Some of you will buy it on your own, and some of you will be handed this book by someone who loves you. Regardless of how you came about this book, just know that the following pages contain the questions that will help you reshape, reform, and reignite your attitude.

I have always wondered why some people seem to be so positive all the time, and conversely, why some people seem to be so negative all the time. What is the common link between successful businesses, successful relationships, and successful people? The common denominator is a Positive Attitude.

This book is written to help you answer these questions: What is my attitude? What would I like my attitude to be? What process can I go through to actually change the way I think about life, relationships, my successes and my failures? The answers you are searching for can be found within this book, and in the companion book, *The Get Attitude Playbook!* This playbook is your personal journal that, when actively written in and taken seriously, will reshape your attitude, grow your influence, and ignite your destiny.

I am fairly certain this book will be unlike anything you have ever read. It is full of questions, deep questions, questions you have possibly never asked yourself. Many who engage with this book will only able to handle one chapter at a time. It is a book that is not meant to be an "easy read," but a book that is meant to redirect your way of thinking and feeling about life. For maximum impact and results, I encourage you to stay patient and not hurry through it. Can a person really change their attitude and direction in life within an hour or two? Some would argue yes; however, lasting and sustainable change and improvement is most attainable when studied and made a priority every day. I invite you to let this book and playbook be your daily guide to lasting change and personal development.

You have taken the first step toward Attitude Realignment by opening this book and beginning your journey. This book will ask you to reflect on your life, discover the root causes of your attitude, face the causes identified, challenge them, and conquer them. This can be painful for some, and freeing for others. I believe it will all depend on your attitude!

The questions and thought processes that are required to transform your attitude should cause you some pain, frustration, and possibly the desire to give up as we go through this book. This is natural, just as natural as you may feel when a physical trainer pushes you in a gym, demanding one more rep, one more push-up. No Pain, No Gain. I ask that you challenge yourself to think, feel, and engage with your past and your present, in order to shape your future.

Ever since the first grade, I've been told there are things that I cannot do, cannot accomplish, or cannot be. I have always been a person who challenges authority and makes his own way. I remember in the sixth grade, my teacher told me that I was on a one-way road to prison. I knew I wasn't going to follow the path that she set out for me. Rather than follow someone else's dead-end road, I made my own path to success and abundance.

I don't know what it was inside of me, if it was how my parents or older siblings raised me, or if it was simply an innate gift from God that I always thought for myself and never let anyone get inside my head. I later learned to call this innate "gift," or "ability," Attitude.

The book you are about to read was inspired by my personal journey through life so far. It reveals how I came to achieve the unachievable and overcome the impossible.

If you are a person who has been told similar things, or if you are a person who has been telling yourself these things, then this book is meant for you. It is meant to free you from your self-limiting thoughts, beliefs, and perceptions.

It has been said, "the way you perceive others affects them, and the way others perceive you, affects you."

I am here to tell you, there is no stronger pull in life than the way you perceive yourself!

When it comes to attitude or personal development programs, people often think there is nothing new to be learned. For the most part, that is true. Presenting old information in a new way, however, can often unlock the truth. Instead of saying, "yeah, I know all this information," you need to ask yourself, "how good am I at practicing it?"

This book will help you redefine your perception and unlock your ability to reinvent, re-engage and re-ignite yourself.

If this interests you, keep reading!

INTRODUCTION

*"If you want things to change,
you must change."*

\- Jim Rohn

Have you ever heard the saying "ATTITUDE is...EVERYTHING"?

As I interview thousands of successful people, coaches, and business leaders, they typically answer "yes" to that question. But when I ask how much they have studied their attitude, taken a course on attitude, or worked on their attitude, I get a look of confusion and concern.

It is amazing how many of us find it easy to identify another person's attitude as being poor or negative, yet when faced with examining our own attitude, we seem to claim ours is "just fine," "no work needed," "no studying, reading books or attending seminars is necessary." "My attitude rocks," is what we say to ourselves.

If challenged about our attitude, we tend to get a bit defensive and say things like, "How dare you challenge my attitude!"

This book is not about me, or anyone else, judging, manipulating or trying to change your attitude. The fact that you picked up this book tells me you are among a small percentage of people whose attitude may be just fine! However, we can all benefit from reflecting upon, improving, and adjusting our attitude so that it can be the best it can be.

I was advised that I should fill this book full of stories and examples of other people and how their attitudes helped them to achieve, triumph, and succeed in life and relationships. Well, that is NOT what you will find in the coming pages.

In fact, I have chosen to write this book with the complete opposite focus, a focus not on other's stories, but on the most important story in your life. The story that causes you to do what you do, think how you think, and feel how you feel. It is called YOUR story. This book is about YOUR story, no one else's. This book is for you and you only. It has been written in order to help you think about your story. It has been written to help you improve how you are feeling about your story. It includes a *Get Attitude Playbook* in order to identify your story and improve it.

The following pages will take you on an adventure of your attitude. There are many different definitions of attitude, and I have my own. **Attitude is simply the way you dedicate yourself to the way you think. I like to take it a step further. How are you feeling about the way you think? Is the way you think giving you everything you want out of life?**

I know already some of you have your guard up and are ready to posture and disagree, judge and close your mind. Perhaps you are already formulating thoughts on how this definition isn't the correct definition or how there is a better one out there.

I know when it comes to this thing called attitude, people are full of their own opinions, full of their own judgements, and full of their own stories about their attitude and the attitudes of others.

For those of you who are open and ready to adjust, develop and improve your attitude, let's work with this definition and move forward through the book.

For those of you in the first group, let go and come back to this definition of attitude after you have worked through this book and see if I have not made my point.

How did I arrive at this definition? It is called life, my story (which isn't as important as your life and your story).

I have seen very smart people fail because they have a poor attitude.

I have seen very rich people go broke because they possessed a poor attitude.

I have seen very successful people crash because of a poor attitude.

I have seen perfectly healthy people become sick or die because of a poor attitude.

How important is attitude? It has the power to change your life for the better or for the worse, the great thing is...YOU get to decide, only you; no one else!

This is why YOUR story;
how you work on YOUR story,
how you perceive YOUR story,
and how you are willing to adjust,
alter and improve YOUR story matters.

This book is about you, your story and rewriting your story through this road called Attitude and its vehicle the *Get Attitude Playbook*. This *Playbook* will become your Attitude journal.

This book was written so you can adjust, analyze, improve and develop the following:

1. Your story
2. Your perceptions about your story
3. Your actions
4. Your perceptions about your actions
5. Your feelings
6. Your perceptions about those feelings (what you think about how you feel)
7. Your thoughts
8. Your perceptions about those thoughts (how you feel about your thoughts)
9. YOUR ATTITUDE

This is not just a book. This is an adventure, a challenge and an interactive formula in order for you to "GET ATTITUDE".

I will further explain in the book what "GET ATTITUDE" means, but for the simplest explanation, I defer to my sister Molly who helpfully described what I do to help others "Get Attitude." She states:

"You work with people to transform their minds and motivate their souls by changing/inspiring a better attitude - a more productive attitude - you are trying to take them from a place of complacency to achievement and success."
- Molly Rondeau

Well said, sis. If what this description says is appealing to you, please keep reading; I think you will be happy!

In the coming pages, you will be challenged to think about your attitude, feel how your attitude is affecting your decisions, relationships and life, be asked to journal and create new and improved thoughts and feelings on paper, and best of all, be directed to take action, which will cause you to manifest your improved attitude in the world for the betterment of others.

My goal is simple for you. After reading and working through this book, you will become a more contagious and attractive person for the betterment of all the people you meet.

The quality of your life is influenced by the quality of the questions you ask about your life. I like to provoke thought and improvement through the use of quality questions. One pivotal question that used to run my life was, "What does can't mean?" I used to ask myself this question all the time, especially in times of great decision making and stress. I found this to be a question which allowed me to achieve greatness in many areas, but it also opened up avenues for destruction and pain that did not benefit the masses, only me. This, in short, was a negative attitude I possessed. By asking this question, I was able to identify an aspect of my life that needed an attitude adjustment.

Once I started asking myself this next question, everything changed for me.

> *"How can I move myself and others from can't to can in a loving and constructive manner?"*

Do you see how just changing the way you ask yourself questions can redirect your life? It did for me. This question created an improved attitude which allowed me to flourish and actually write this book.

Having an Amazing Attitude is as simple as the ABC's; however, getting there may not be easy. It will take work, daily work, and dedication to yourself to do the activities this book requires of you. Analyzing, rewriting and improving your story will take hard work, intense thinking and an open mind when it comes to how you feel about where you are.

However, I will guarantee you this is the best source for attitude adjustment, development and attitude improvement available to you, the most important attitude in the world.

Change and improvement always starts with you!

I say, "If you want your life to change, then you must change your attitude. You must change the way you think, think about how you feel, and change the way you feel about how you think."

This book is your guide to doing that; it is YOUR story that matters most, so let's begin your journey and create your secret formula to your Amazing Attitude.

Throughout this book, at the end of each chapter and with each Alphabet Attitude Challenge, you will be presented with Attitude Transformation Opportunities. You'll be asked to take out your *Get Attitude Playbook* and write down your responses to thought provoking questions. With this tool, you will begin to transform your attitude into what I call an Amazing Attitude.

Download your *Get Attitude Playbook* now at
www.abcsofattitude.com
and begin your attitude transformation!

Attitude Transformation Opportunity - Go to your *Get Attitude Playbook* and write down your responses to these questions.

- In times of great stress and decision making, what questions am I asking myself most often? What is your pivotal question?

- Is there a different question that would change my attitude or actions if I just found it and asked it? What is that question?

Part One

Get Attitude!

GOALS

- Learn the definition of attitude!
- Learn what it means to Get Attitude!
- Learn the RID OF Formula!
- Get started with your attitude transformation!

Chapter 1

Its Time to GET ATTITUDE

*"Attitude is a little thing
that makes a big difference."*
- Winston Churchill

Many people have trouble wrapping their head around the concept of "GET ATTITUDE." Some say it sounds negative, some say it sounds impossible, others say they have no idea what it really means.

When I say "Get Attitude" all I mean is you need to become in control of your thought process. Increase your control, your focus, your intentions regarding your attitude toward your health, your relationships, your finances, and ultimately the direction of your life.

Let's face it, most people are not dedicated to a way of thinking when it comes to their health, their relationships, their finances and their life. People are very casual and let all these areas just "happen," they react daily in each area depending on who or what stimulus prods them into doing so.

Having an Amazing Attitude means that you are dedicated to dictating these areas of your life, not living in a mode of reaction to these. In other words, most people wait until health and/or financial ruin sets in before they consider a change or consider "Getting Attitude" regarding those areas. Some wait for divorce papers to show up before they "Get Attitude" and fix their marriage or relationships.

"Getting Attitude" puts you in front, it helps you lead your life, instead of just being dragged along only to react to circumstances when it is too late. Parents wonder why their kids get so messed up, or get into "the wrong crowd." It is simple; they are hanging around a peer group that has attitude, but their attitude is not one of "prosperous productivity." Parents can encourage and model "prosperous productivity" by evaluating their own thoughts while they encourage their children to examine their beliefs and think for themselves. If parents only "Get Attitude," then their children would have someone to look up to, to model, to follow. Most don't, and as I see it, that is the number 1 contributor to why kids struggle with attitude.

Attitude is best broken down into two parts, by identifying the way you:

1. Feel about how you think.

We all have thoughts; a way of thinking that determines our attitude. At times, however, we should ask ourselves, "Is what I am thinking true? Even if it is true, why is it that what I am thinking makes me "feel" so uncomfortable, uneasy, or uncertain?" There are times we need to step back and take an inventory of how we are thinking, and ask the following questions in order to get "attitude alignment" with our emotions. If you are thinking a certain way about a situation, occurrence or relationship, and that train of thought makes you "feel" negative, helpless or angry, you should take time to evaluate your negative reactions. Think about one negative or stressful situation, occurrence, or relationship, and ask yourself the following questions:

1. Am I okay feeling this, why?
2. What does it say about me to feel this way?
3. Does this feeling show a sign of weakness, why?
4. Does this feeling show a sign of strength or empowerment, why?
5. How or why will others find these feelings attractive and empowering to them?
6. How will these feelings solve problems, offer solutions or bridge the gap?

"Attitude Alignment" is simply when your way of thinking and your emotions are congruent; they are in line. I believe when your thoughts and emotions/feelings are on the same track, you become a person of massive impact and action. Understand living in conflict between what you think and what you feel will not be conducive to an Amazing Attitude.

Your answers to these questions you will see are NOT "reasons" or "excuses." They are "challenges" or "motivators" which will propel and pull you forward through any obstacle. These are the answers that employers, business partners, venture capitalists and anyone associating with you will grab onto and say, "This is a person I want to have in my business or life."

Are you this type of person? Attitude is contagious, attractive and influential. Studying it will make you a person who people feel addicted to, attracted to and worthy of being influenced by.

I have never seen a person with a bad
attitude get the opportunities in life that
a person with a good attitude gets!

2. Think about how you feel.

How we think about what we feel implies that we feel automatically about certain things, events, occurrences or actions in our lives. There are inherent responses (feelings) to stimulus that auto-generate when they enter our life. When "things" happen to us, for us, or about us, we instantly feel an emotion and make decisions and take actions based on that instantaneous reflex. Not all of us, but most of us, are creatures of emotional response. Have you ever said to yourself, "Why did I do that?" or "That was just not me!" You say these things because you had no "attitude alignment" between your feelings and your thoughts.

Attitude alignment comes into this equation when we STOP and think about what we are feeling and why. Most people associate attitude with emotion, but it actually is more so tied to THINKING rather than feeling. So, to get to the bottom of this, "How we think about what we feel" is a process that interrupts acting immediately on our emotions, this process of "How we think about what we feel" is started by asking the following questions:

1. Why am I feeling this way?
2. What beliefs must I have to be feeling this way?
3. What has to be true that I would automatically feel this way?
4. Is what I am feeling the truth?
5. Is what I am feeling leading me toward avoiding pain or seeking pleasure?
6. How must I dedicate my way of thinking that will allow me the most powerful, impactful and positive result for myself and others?

Your answers to these questions will best be defined as the "reasons" you are the way you are or do things the way you do them.

I don't care what problem, challenge or obstacle you are facing; they are making you feel certain emotions. How you think through those emotions will influence how people who are decision makers, teammates, family, and friends will respond to you. If you want to dictate their response, your Amazing Attitude will lead the way.

Attitude Transformation Opportunity - Go to your *Get Attitude Playbook* and write down your answers to the questions presented in this chapter.

Feel about how you think -

Think about one negative or stressful situation, occurrence, or relationship, and ask yourself:

- Am I okay feeling this, why?
- What does it say about me to feel this way?
- Does this feeling show a sign of weakness, why?
- Does this feeling show a sign of strength or empowerment, why?
- How or why will others find these feelings attractive and empowering to them?
- How will these feelings solve problems, offer solutions or bridge the gap?

Think about how you feel -

- Why am I feeling this way?
- What beliefs must I have to be feeling this way?

- What has to be true that I would automatically feel this way?
- Is what I am feeling the truth?
- Is what I am feeling leading me toward avoiding pain or seeking pleasure?
- How must I dedicate my way of thinking that will allow me the most powerful, impactful and positive result for myself and others?

Chapter 2

RID OF Formula

"The only disability in life is a bad attitude."
- Scott Hamilton

I have developed the formula to "Get Attitude." It is called the **RID OF Formula.** It is meant to help you get RID OF complacency, unhappiness, lethargy, bad health, bad habits, and most of all, your BAD ATTITUDE. It is a process that will get you to begin to dedicate yourself to a way of thought and could quite possibly turn it all around for you.

If you are tired of all the negativity in your life, all the lack of vitality in your health and relationships, and lastly, the feelings and realization that there is a better you inside, then use this formula to GET ATTITUDE!

R - RECOGNIZE your negative thought patterns (attitude) when it comes to whatever you want to change about your behavior or results. Truly identify how you think about it and why you think that way. Then go a little deeper and ask yourself, how do I feel about what I think? Why am I thinking this way? Why am I feeling this way? Unless, you become honest and recognize your negative thoughts and feelings toward a person, situation or occurrence you cannot begin to GET ATTITUDE and breakthrough.

I - IDENTIFY how these challenges (attitudes) limit your life. This step sounds easy. It is easy to talk and think about it to yourself, but I suggest you write it down. Then it sticks. The reality of what you are costing yourself becomes more tangible. I don't care what it is, if you have a bad attitude about something, then that is costing you, somehow someway. Questions that you can ask yourself to identify what a negative or bad attitude is costing you are the following:

1. What would be possible if I changed my attitude about this?
2. What am I not getting in a physical or emotional sense when it comes to this challenge and my attitude about this challenge?
3. Who else would benefit or appreciate it if I changed my attitude?
4. How is this limiting my life?
5. Am I a better more productive person having a negative attitude toward this challenge?

Search and find what the cost to you is, then write it down, stare at it and go to step three, Decide.

D - DECIDE you must change! Tony Robbins taught me this great saying, "Convert those "shoulds" into "musts" and your entire life changes." So will your attitude. Many of us have attitude or thought processes that we feel we should change, but we don't. Why? Because we don't feel we **must** change. The R & I parts of this formula set you up to recognize and identify what you should do. The Decision part of the equation is where the attitude achievers and the attitude wishers separate. It is the difference between success and failure in any part of your life. Tony Robbins also points out that, "It is in your moments of decision that your destiny is created." **I believe that it is in moments of decision about your attitude, your way of thinking, that change the direction and course of your life forever.** Look around at the countless examples of what people have accomplished when they just DECIDED to!

O - Overcome your excuses and take action. The very natural response to making a decision that you are uncomfortable with, or don't believe in, will be for you to start to create excuses that will turn your "musts" right back into "shoulds." Taking action will immediately curb your instinct to rationalize and wither in your attempt to change your life and attitude. Actions can involve mostly state changes (physical), sense changes (smell, taste, hear), or lastly emotional changes, focusing on the power of your feelings and seeing yourself already accomplishing a new way of thought or task. **To Overcome is an attitude unto itself.** It seems every day, every hour, almost every minute, we are constantly battling what society, the media and people close to us are trying to get us to think. **Everyone wants a piece of your mind; when you do not overcome that, those forces now have the ability to dictate your way of thinking and create a new way for you to dedicate yourself to the way THEY think, not you.**

Ask yourself, at the end of the day, how many people did I let dictate their way of thought into my life and my actions? I am not saying it is bad to let those of higher attitude achievement, personal achievement and business achievement into your mind space, but the person who has the quick ability to recognize an "attitude sucker" is imperative. An "attitude sucker" is a person who sucks the positive attitude right out of you. They are people who will read this book and argue, correct and break out in hives with some of these philosophies. An attitude to Overcome is one of the greatest gifts I can give you in this book. Be an overcomer, not an under-comer.

F - Faithfulness to your attitude. I never want to get too religious in my books, but I am a very religious person. I will allow myself a simple reference to the higher power of faith in this book. I don't care what religion you are, but being a person of faith matters. Being a person of faith about your attitude matters. You must have belief and faith that after you have gone through this book, done the journaling and really reflected on your attitude that you will faithfully carry out all the wonderful things you have discovered, planned and dreamed about. It is tough to shake a person's faith, just like it should be tough to shake a person's attitude. I am here to tell you that faith in your attitude should be just as important as your faith in your higher power. So many people have weak attitudes because they have weak faith and belief in their attitude. Why? Most people never take the time to study attitude, search for attitude or develop their attitude. When you finally take the time to do these things, then stand firm to what you have learned and never stop learning and developing. Just as you can never read the Bible, Koran or any other book that leads a religion, you should never stop studying your attitude. Yes, it is okay to think of your attitude as a religion. In the sense that one should never stop studying it, developing it, and sharing positive attitude with others.

Attitude Transformation Opportunity - Go to your *Get Attitude Playbook* and use the RID OF Formula to identify the negative attitudes that you need to get rid of. Reflect upon and write down your answers to the questions that were presented in this chapter.

- How do I feel about what I think?
- Why am I thinking this way?
- Why am I feeling this way?

- What would be possible if I changed my attitude about this?
- What am I not getting in a physical or emotional sense when it comes to this challenge and my attitude about this challenge?
- Who else would benefit or appreciate it if I changed my attitude?
- How is this limiting my life?
- Am I a better more productive person having a negative attitude toward this challenge?
- At the end of the day, how many people did I let dictate their way of thought into my life and my actions?

Search and find what your negative attitude is costing you, then write it down, stare at it, and process it. **Until you identify the consequences of a negative attitude, you can't make the changes needed to get an Amazing Attitude!**

Chapter 3

The 3 Biggest Mistakes to Avoid for an Amazing Attitude

*"The greatest discovery of any generation
is that a human being can alter his life
by altering his attitude."*

-William James

So many people wonder if you are born with a good attitude or is it something that is learned?

Well, the honest answer is a little bit of both. If you were fortunate enough to be raised by parents or caregivers who possessed a good or positive attitude, you probably have been conditioned to view the world from the perspective of having a good attitude. On the other hand, if you were raised by parents and/or people who had a negative attitude or a poor attitude, that would certainly explain the reasons for how you look at the world and how you dedicate yourself to the way you think.

Remember, my definition for attitude is how you feel about what you think or what you think about how you feel. Regardless, there is a process of conscious thought that is linked to attitude.

Without thought, you are just left with emotion, raw and real. Emotion by itself is just emotion, it is NOT your attitude. Your attitude is the filter, if you will, that you run your emotions through. Your emotions either get filtered in a positive light or a negative one. They get filtered with a positive outlook or meaning and/or a negative one. To determine if you have a positive attitude or a negative one, all you really need to do is stop and think, or write down, what comes into your mind or to your lips when you are interacting with others. If you take the time to do this and you actually read what you are thinking, it will become quite clear if you have a negative or positive attitude.

The challenge is this, can you find the positive in everything that crosses your desk, your relationships and your mind? If you work on it and dedicate yourself to it the answer is YES!

However, there are reasons why the average person will not take the time to do this. There are mistakes that people make when it comes to their attitude. I love to ask my audiences, "Do you think your attitude could use a little adjusting?" Very seldom do people raise their hand and answer yes. Then I ask, "Is there someone in your life whose attitude could use a little adjusting?" Man, do the hands literally fly up. The reality is someone is wrong, either you or everyone else. If you think that everyone around you needs an attitude adjustment, but your's is perfectly fine, you are in denial.

I have identified what seems to be the three biggest mistakes people make when it comes to their attitude. People make these mistakes even when they agree to study, improve and get their needed attitude adjustment.

The solution to getting a positive attitude, or obtaining an attitude adjustment for the good, is as easy as the ABC's. Identifying the biggest mistakes is also as easy as the ABC's!

MISTAKE NUMBER 1
ADDICTION TO YOUR ATTITUDE

Addiction is one of the most predominant obstacles in many people's lives. Most people are addicted to something: alcohol, cigarettes, food, TV, video games, and cell phones. Perhaps the biggest addiction of all, that is undiagnosed in many, perhaps never studied or surveyed, is the addiction to our own lousy attitude. People are addicted to the way they think, the way they feel about how they think, and what they think. They hold on to their attitudes as tight as a mother holds on to her newborn child. People don't know why they aren't willing to change or improve their attitude, they just know they don't want to. They think they are comfortable with it, it supplies them many reasons to stay in the status quo, to not change, not grow, not experience life to its fullest. If I don't need to change my attitude, then I don't need to change, period.

However, a problem exists: if you are not growing, then you are dying. People do not ever stay the same. They are changing for the better or the worse every day. This change is not obvious, it is subtle. It is so subtle that it becomes the downfall of many of us; it creeps up on us like a thug and knocks us over the head when it is too late. So, are you addicted to your attitude? Well, if you have not investigated your attitude, studied your attitude, or read a book on attitude, then my guess is yes! Thankfully, you now have this book and you are on your way to an attitude adjustment that will be long term. You are on a new journey to freer thinking, empowering thinking and self-discovery that will make you stronger, more decisive and more pleasant to be around. **Attitude is attractive and contagious; get some and ride the wave.**

MISTAKE NUMBER 2 - BAD BELIEFS

So much of our attitude depends on what we believe. I love to ask the question, "Is everything you believe true?" I then ask the next question, "Is what everybody else believes true?" Then the third question, "Is everything everybody else believes about you true?" Well, when processing these three questions, both parties can't be right, somebody has got to be wrong, either you or them. I will submit to you the idea that there are certainly a few things that you are believing that aren't true. I will also submit that there are beliefs everyone else has that are not true, lastly, I am fairly certain there are beliefs others have about you that are not true. These falsehoods drive our behavior, our thoughts and our attitudes. Not only ours, but the thoughts and behaviors of others towards us. When we have "bad beliefs" or self-limiting thought, or when we let others impose their "bad beliefs" on us, it is next to impossible to have positive creative thought, which is a foundation for a positive attitude.

MISTAKE NUMBER 3
(The) CAN'T CONUNDRUM

The biggest mistake most people make when it comes to their attitude is their focus. **You feel what you focus on.** Most people focus on the negative. They focus on what they can't be, do, or have. They focus on who they are not, or even worse, they focus and envy other people's success. They become envious of those who have, and they are never joyful or proud of the people in their lives who are succeeding.

It is virtually impossible to cultivate, maintain and sustain a positive, Amazing Attitude when your focus and self-talk involves the word can't. Again, the challenge is just as we did with the beliefs; eliminate the word can't from your vocabulary. What is that word really doing to inspire you, help you flourish and most of all keep you happy and positive? Once you eliminate it from your vocabulary, you will soon begin to listen clearer to those around you and see who suffers from the can't conundrum.

Attitude Transformation Opportunity - Go to your *Get Attitude Playbook* and identify if you feel addicted to your attitude. If so, why?

- What other addictions do you have that are compromising your attitude?
- Identify the ten beliefs that you are holding on to that are not serving your growth, happiness and success. Write them down and then and smash them, leave them on the paper, and extract them from your mind.

Go ahead and replace them with them with new true (or soon to be), empowering beliefs, your attitude will shine and so will you!

Part Two

Smashing Your Lousy Attitude is as Easy as the ABC's!

GOALS

Continue your Attitude transformation by:

- Accepting the 26 Alphabet Attitude Challenges!
- Answering thought provoking questions in your *Get Attitude Playbook!*

Chapter 4

Attitude Basics

"Motivation is just like bathing,
it is something we recommend you do daily."
- Zig Ziglar

Attitude improvement is much like bathing, it is something we recommend you do everyday!

Now that you are aware of the three biggest mistakes to avoid when it comes to having an Amazing Attitude, it is time for you to get some answers and tools in order to keep your attitude... AMAZING!

Do you ever notice how some people in your life just seem to simply have an amazing attitude all the time? How are they able to do that? Is it natural? Well, for some people it is because of their DNA and upbringing. There are also people who actually work and focus on having an amazing attitude.

The great Zig Ziglar answered the question about motivation and how to stay motivated this way, "Motivation is just like bathing, it is something we recommend you do daily." If not, the stink will build up and you can get what we call "stinkin' thinkin'."

My guess is when you think of the most positive people who are in your life, the ones you look at and say, "My gosh, they get it; I'd love to have an attitude like them!", chances are they are practicing one, if not all, of these at some point in their day. If they are really good, my guess is they are starting their day with one of these tools or Challenges as I call them.

Before you get these Alphabet Attitude Challenges it is important to understand that attitude comes in two forms…Positive and Negative. I see no reason to focus on negative attitudes, or how people get them, because I know of no person who has asked me to help develop their negative attitude! So, as we show you these 26 Alphabet Attitude Challenges, they are meant to help you gravitate toward, pull through and master having a good attitude.

Understand this: having, owning, learning about, cultivating and possessing a positive attitude is all about you and your desire to achieve one. I cannot force you, you cannot force anyone else, it's a choice, it's a choice most people with a negative attitude are not equipped to make, don't understand and are helpless in their pursuit on their own. That is why I wrote this book, as a simple easy guide for those who are closed and stuck in their circumstance not their vision to breakout and live a life of happiness, contribution, significance and certainty in their own head. It may sound a bit overwhelming, all these good things, but I can assure you they are better than having despair, uncertainty, loneliness, self-pity and boredom in your life.

So, if you want to have an Amazing Attitude,
it is as easy as the ABC's!

With each Alphabet Attitude Challenge, you will be presented with Attitude Transformation Opportunities. You'll be asked to take out your *Get Attitude Playbook* and write down your responses to thought provoking questions. With this tool, you will begin to transform your attitude into what I call an Amazing Attitude.

Download your *Get Attitude Playbook* now at
www.abcsofattitude.com
and begin your attitude transformation!

A - Attitude Awareness!

Awareness is the opposite of Attitude Addiction. So many people who struggle with addiction have no idea how they are acting or what drives them to do what they do. They are helpless in their own mind and have no idea or awareness about what and how their actions influence the lives of those who love them, and more importantly they don't recognize how they are destroying their own life. Attitude awareness is just like the first step in the 12 steps to recovery. Admitting, "I am powerless over alcohol" is like a person saying that their negative attitude is like an addiction. It is driven in their psyche and they must first become more aware of what their negative attitude has cost them and what adjusting that attitude could mean for their happiness and overall success. Becoming aware of your attitude is not easy, this is the toughest and deepest step, but until we get past the A, we can't go to B.

It has been said that your attitude is like a bank, and you need to have five positive thoughts for every negative thought. A positive thought counts as one credit in your attitude bank; a negative thought costs you five debits. A negative attitude is five times more powerful on you than a positive attitude. Why do people usually default to the negative? It helps you avoid pain which is the biggest driver of humans. Example: I need to call a prospect today, they are probably busy or don't want to be called. So, one more day won't hurt. You must consciously choose to be positive, stay positive and filter positive in every human contact you know by at least 5 to 1. This formula will keep you on track and guarantee you an amazing attitude.

To be Aware just simply means to take an inventory of what you say, how you are saying it, and consciously keep a little record. Try it for a day, then a week then a month, and see if you are aware of how you are showing up for yourself and others. I compare Awareness to a light. Without it, you are in the dark and you will be susceptible to where other attitudes lead you, market to you and manipulate your feelings and emotions. Get aware so you can be independent and lead rather than follow.

Attitude Transformation Opportunity - Go to your *Get Attitude Playbook* and fill in the blanks in in the following sentences and write down your answers to the questions.

- The three biggest opportunities my attitude has cost me are _____ , _____ , _____ .
- What did I need to believe in order to possess this attitude and how can I come to believe any different?
- If I had a more positive attitude about _____ , what would the benefits be to myself and those around me who I care about?
- What would I have to believe in order to bring this attitude into my life for good?

B - Be Nice!

We have known for a long time that being nice is the number 1 way to boost your attitude! Have you ever tried walking through a day and being nice? I mean overly nice to everybody you come in contact with. I say try it and you will feel what an Amazing Attitude can do for you and, more importantly, others. We know psychologically and physiologically that being nice improves your health, so why not try it?

Is it easier to be mean and negative than be nice? Some would say yes; I would agree. Humans always seem to default to negative, not nice attitudes and behaviors. I wrote this book to help people become more aware of this fact and to ultimately figure out a way that we create a community of people where the default is set on nice and positive rather than mean and negative. Which type of community would you rather live in?

Attitude Transformation Opportunity - Go to your *Get Attitude Playbook* and write down the last three times you were mean and negative.

- Identify if you were better off in each circumstance.
- Now, write down how you could have responded in a nice and positive way and how that outcome could have changed.
- Identify when being negative and mean cost you. What did it cost?
- Identify when being nice benefited you.

**Recognize the benefits of kindness and
continue to ride the nice train.**

C - **Control Your Emotions!**

As I speak around the country, I ask my audiences two questions:

- How would you describe your attitude in two words or less?
- What would you like your attitude to be?

The number one answer I get on question number 2 is CONSISTENT. I then point out that it is hard to have a consistent attitude with inconsistent emotions. Think about the time you made the biggest mistake in your life. Were your emotions in control or out of control? The ability to control your emotions is a tough, conscious decision one must undertake in order to keep a more consistent attitude in an effort to make it amazing. I am not telling you to not be emotional, it is only natural that you are, but being at full tilt emotionally ten or more times a day will not make you attractive or contagious, and it certainly won't classify you as having a contagious, Amazing Attitude. Flying off the handle is not just an outward practice but an inward discontent and anxiety that you feel eating away at you.

Attitude Transformation Opportunity - Go to your *Get Attitude Playbook* and write down your answers to these questions.

- How well do I control my attitude and emotions?
- Do I fly off the handle?
- If I do, will I commit to record such occurrences so as to measure my ability to control my emotions?

D - Do More than You are Paid For!

I realize that many people who are reading this book are well paid, highly educated, and have already reached success on this principle; however, my guess is that you know someone in your life who isn't. In fact, when we look at the truly wealthy and successful, that encompasses only about 3% of the US population. Doing more than what you are paid for is the essence of "moving up the ladder" both in personal income and personal development. This is a principle that unleashes ultimate power and creates an awareness, attractiveness and contagiousness towards you that will not go unnoticed. The quickest way up the ladder is to constantly outperform yourself, your peers and your boss's expectations.

You will be found, but you must commit, you must believe, and you must act when the opportunity presents itself. You need to be AWARE and always looking for the person who sees you actively engaged and doing more than expected. Maybe you have done more than you were paid for, but feel that your extra work went unrecognized, unappreciated and unrewarded. I would challenge you that the receiver of your actions only felt that you were doing what they expected. Expectations are a funny thing, and if not clearly defined, you will always have problems. Lack of consistency and understanding of expectations will ruin the attitude of both the employer and the employee.

Attitude Transformation Opportunity - Go to your *Get Attitude Playbook* and write down your answers to these questions.

- When was the last time I did more than I was paid for?
- How did it make me feel? Was it worth it? Was I recognized? Was it really MORE than I was paid for?

- When did a lack of clarity of expectations ruin my attitude?
- When I did have clarity of expectations, how much more did I enjoy my task, mission, career, or relationship?

Chapter 5

Attitude Explosion

E - Effort!

The secret to life, happiness, and success, and the title of my next book. Let's just say Jim Rohn was right, "Success is a few simple disciplines practiced every day." The measure of success is doing one simple thing every day to better your life. That kind of discipline takes effort, but it is well worth it. Put effort into your relationships and your health. Your EFFORT is the biggest gamble you can take with your time, some bet more than others. When I look at the successful people in my life, their willingness to gamble their time and effort toward a goal far supercedes those who don't have the time or give the effort. **Success doesn't just fall out of a tree and hit you on the head. It is earned through the investment of time and the focus of effort.**

"E" is such a great letter with attitude, I just have to add a few words and thoughts under "E."

Enthusiasm! If you are not excited about your life, your job, your spouse, your friends and your family, then I feel sorry for you. Enthusiasm, just like attitude, is contagious and attractive. The more enthusiastic you are, the more people will want to help you succeed. Especially if you are enthusiastic about them. How enthusiastic are you about all your relationships?

Eat Right and Exercise! I mean really! Does this surprise you? It is amazing to me the hundreds of millions that are spent on marketing diets, pills, paying for people to simply weigh you in, personal trainers, video workouts and even gym memberships. I get all of it and hope you buy it. For exercise, I recommend looking at what Jack LaLanne, "the godfather of fitness", does and you will be GOLD.

Let me tell you what I've learned about exercise, diet and nutrition. Eat fruits and vegetables only for one month. Walk a minimum of a mile a day and increase it one mile every week. You will lose weight and feel great. If you want to throw a little chicken in, do it, fish, do it. Trust me, it will work. Now the hard part, no alcohol, sugars, or preservatives, and stay away from white powders. This is not revolutionary, but it is easy: eat right and exercise.

Energy! Simple formula, people who have massive energy are Eating right, Exercising more, and Enthusiastic about their life!

Attitude Transformation Opportunity - Go to your *Get Attitude Playbook* and write down your answers to these questions.

- What can I do to bring more energy and enthusiasm into my life?
- What simple disciplines can I practice every day to improve my health, and ultimately, my attitude?

F - Focus!

You feel what you focus on. Think about it. Thinking is the biggest part of attitude. When you feel down and out, lonely, sad, or excluded, all you are thinking about are circumstances that make you feel that way or present themselves to you that way. How fast does it take to change your focus? Well, in my world, one second. If you are feeling down, I suggest you change your focus immediately. I once heard from Tony Robbins that suicide and depression occur from focusing on what you don't have, constantly. This is not healthy and does not enable you to have a great attitude. I agree with him that, **"Developing a habit of appreciating what you have can create a new level of emotional well-being and wealth."**[1] Catch yourself when feeling down, what are you thinking?

Attitude Transformation Opportunity - Go to your *Get Attitude Playbook* and write down your answers to this question.

What are the three things I can always focus on that change my attitude immediately? These three things will change, but they are real and you need to use them to create a way of thinking that does not allow you to focus on negative thoughts.

> Focus on what you do have, what you are grateful for and what gifts you bring to others.

G - Grow or Die!

The great Coach Lou Holtz, once said, "You are either Growing or Dying, you never stay the same." I have never met a person with a great attitude that has not experienced, read, or watched new information in order for them to grow. In fact, most miserable people are stuck in a rut. They are stuck in their circumstance and they let people define them, including themselves, by their circumstances. You have been provided a huge list of resources in the back of this book that will help you grow. As stated in the

---

[1]   "The 3 Decisions That Will Change Your Financial Life." 2014. 6 Jul. 2015 <http://www.entrepreneur.com/article/239312>

Bible, "Seek, and ye shall find." If you are not seeking to grow, you are seeking to die. If you are reading this book, I know you are the former not the latter, so congratulations!

Attitude Transformation Opportunity - Go to your *Get Attitude Playbook* and write down your answers to these questions. Everyone has strengths and room for growth.

- What is something that I would like to learn?
- How would this help me grow as a person?

H - Have a Big Goal!

Even if you feel your goals are unattainable, unreachable and not realistic, there is still value in dreaming big and setting outrageous goals. You may think them impossible, but I have seen those with Amazing Attitudes have their unattainable, unrealistic goals actually come to fruition in their lifetime. Limitless goal setting is a difficult exercise, but man is it fun! Surprise yourself. You can imagine the biggest, most crazy goals; never doubt that they can come true. Ask the universe; you may be surprised at the answer you get. Stop listening to goal setters who believe in limits and quantify them as attainable.

I have done thousands of goal setting sessions; here are some of the few things I have learned.

- The mind is a goal seeking device.
- The more you see and speak your goal, the greater likelihood you will hit it. Do not just mention your goal every day, but focus on it every hour.
- Those who expect double, and learn how to set a goal for more than they ever dreamed, tend to hit it.

- There are formulas and workshops and work sheets, but just get three big goals and become obsessed with them.
- Don't ask how, just ask why. When the why becomes big enough, the how gets taken care of.
- You believe; impose your will on that goal. No one else will, so don't ask for help. They are all looking at you jealously because of your fearlessness.
- Double your goal and don't worry about, calculate, or plan on how to achieve it. The supernatural powers of your mind and the universe will take you there. How in the world do you think I ended up writing this book?

I have reinvented the old SMART Goal formula to capture and create your BIG GOALS! SPECIFIC, MEASURABLE, ACTIONABLE, ROMANTIC, TIMELY

The old SMART Goal formula (specific, measurable, attainable, realistic, timely) is useful, practical and recommended, so I am including it in this book. That goal setting formula is for another time and purpose. Obviously, the biggest difference in my formula eliminate the ceiling with the ACTIONABLE and ROMANTIC features.

Attitude Transformation Opportunity - Go to your *Get Attitude Playbook* and list your most outrageous goals. Don't worry about how outrageous and big they are, just write them, expand your mind and don't worry about the feedback you and others may give after you write them down. Truly write a list of what you and others would think to be unattainable in your lifetime. You will surprise yourself. Write down your top three goals now. Make sure to write down the why behind each one. You need to fall in love with your big goal; that is the key! (That is where the Romance comes in).

I - Imitate Greatness!

Ever heard the saying, "Success leaves clues"? Well, this book is loaded with clues for your greatness, and it all starts with your attitude. Who are the people in your life that are successful the way you want to be successful? I always challenge my audiences with this question, "Is there someone in your life, whether you know them or not, who could change the direction of your life drastically if you had the courage to engage them?" They have the clues you desire. Identify these people and approach them for a 30 minute meeting. I have done this and I have brought no less than 100 questions to each meeting. I suggest you do the same. Wouldn't you want to be prepared if, in fact, you met a world leader, media leader, religious leader, movie star because your attitude brought you there? Then get writing!

Attitude Transformation Opportunity - Go to your *Get Attitude Playbook* and answer this question.

- Who are the people in your life that are successful the way you want to be successful? Write the 100 questions that you will ask the people in the world that you can imagine meeting.
- Who are the people not in your life at this time who could change everything for you if you had the courage to engage them? Identify twelve of them. Contact one each month and make it happen. I challenged my good friend Steve, who knew several millionaires, to invite them to lunch, ask them questions, follow the Attitude Engagement Formula, and see where that takes him; you should try that too!
- This doesn't have to be with millionaires, but with people who lead and set the tone in their industry, people who are not just an expert, but THE expert. An expert doesn't

just need to be in business; you can also interview attitude experts, religious leaders, teachers, coaches, police, soldiers, people who give of themselves and are truly underpaid. Their lessons are the greatest of all.

Chapter 6

Attitude Feeling

J - Joy in Adversity!

I love adversity. It makes me feel alive. I pray for adversity; it touches my soul and my faith. How do you respond to adversity? The only people I know who have no adversity are dead. The only people I know who love to complain about their adversity are poor - both in wealth and attitude.

According to American football coach Lou Holtz, "Never tell your problems to anyone…20% don't care and the other 80% are glad you have them." I couldn't agree more!

Not to say that commiseration and venting with a dear, close friend who has read this book is wrong, but defining your life, your attitude and your relationships based on negative thought or adversity makes you a very unattractive non-contagious person. Adversity strengthens the soul. Iron sharpens iron. It makes you tougher, stouter, a deeper person, more humble…need I go on? Adversity is a gift. Treat it like one. Change your attitude about it.

Attitude Transformation Opportunity - Go to your *Get Attitude Playbook* and write about a challenge you are facing and list four reasons why this adversity is of benefit to you. It will change your attitude immediately.

K - Keep On Keepin' On!

This is a familiar saying; however, is this your mentality? Are you a person who is able to finish and deliver on your tasks or promises? If you are not, this lack of "closing" or "delivering the goods" will haunt you, turn you negative, foster a negative attitude and an excuse-laden attitude. Unfinished business is a drag: a drag on your attitude, a drag on your experience and a drag on your reputation. Those who possess the Keep On Keepin' On attitude are patient, focused, and ultimately recognized as doers and people with unbelievable attitudes. Keep On Keepin' On is simply a way of thinking; it is a focus and dedication to your personal and business missions and relationships. "Don't give up, don't ever give up!" - Jimmy Valvano

Attitude Transformation Opportunity - Go to your *Get Attitude Playbook* and list the three most important unfinished items of business, either personal or professional, that you have "not delivered" on, that you have not "kept on keepin' on."

Write down how it will feel to finally finish these tasks, what will your benefits be and how you will feel if these are not finished.

You follow through with these tasks, and I guarantee you, your attitude will boost, you will feel great and you will be proud of your three new accomplishments. From experience, I know it feels amazing; I did this personally while beginning to write this book!

L - LOVE!

Well, this too is obvious. However, do you live in the obvious? Do you even notice the obvious? The Bible tells us that the greatest commandment of all is to "Love." Why, maybe God knew I'd be writing this book; it gives him just one more place to deliver the message. Are you a person of love? Really? How loving are you on a scale of 1 to 10? How would your friends and family rate your ability to love and, more importantly, receive love? If all you set your mind to after reading this book is to be a person of LOVE, I promise you your quest to "get attitude" will become a reality. There have been a million books on Love written, which only confuses the issue. In my opinion, Love is more of a feeling than a mindset, which is why I touch on feeling and thinking in my definition of attitude. It can be debated whether attitude is more based on thinking or feeling; however, I do know this, the most powerful emotion on Earth is the ability to LOVE, and our biggest craving is to be loved by others. Let's just keep it at that. Now that you know the obvious, practice loving and accepting love when it comes your way. It is simple, but not always easy. Walk with love in your heart every minute. Everyone you meet craves the delivery; trust me, it feels better to love than to be loved.

Attitude Transformation Opportunity - Go to your *Get Attitude Playbook* and write down the three people who would benefit most from you showing them more love and the three people who show you love that you take for granted.

How can I acknowledge all six people (maybe less if they are the same) and give and receive to begin to shape
your attitude?

M - Make it Better!

Making improvements is a skill few people have. This takes the ability to assess a situation, identify what is holding that situation back, as well as identify what specific steps it takes to make it better. The fundamental breakdown of any "situation," be it relationship, service, or performance will usually lie in the attitudes of its participants: how they feel about what they are thinking or how they are thinking about what they feel. There is an inconsistency that exists which does not allow them to "make it happen"! If you become a person who is known for making it happen, your value will double and so will your income. In my life, I have found in order to "make things happen" I just go ahead and do it all myself. Why? Because I can direct with single focus on my attitude only and not the attitude of others. Unfortunately, in life, we need others to make it happen. However, the first goal to helping others make it happen is to make it happen for you. What do I mean by "it"? Yes, I mean make your attitude happen. Attitudes are contagious and attractive; others will fall in line once yours is mastered. In other words, I have found the best way to make things happen is to lead by example and the others will follow. Stay above the negative and lead with a positive attitude, trust me they will follow.

Attitude Transformation Opportunity - Go to your *Get Attitude Playbook* and write down two situations, events, or goals that you need to make happen, especially involving other people.

- What are the three things I can do to alter the process and "make it happen"? (Maybe giving all the players this book is a good start!)
- Write down what the number 1 attitude, rule and action that it will take to make it happen…then MAKE IT HAPPEN!

N - Namaste!

Interesting choice for "N", don't you think? I will never forget going into my first yoga class and having my attitude totally adjusted with the thoughts, the process and thinking so 180 degrees different from the way I was wired. It was so natural, so kind, so peaceful, so accepting. Namaste comes from two root words: Nama means to bow, as means "I," and te means "you."[2] Therefore, Namaste literally means "I bow to you." Interesting attitude for sure. Much like "servant leadership." I found that putting myself beneath those who I encounter creates an attractiveness and contagiousness that is on a whole new playing field. Most people call this humility. Humility, which I could have used in "H," is one of the most underused, most contagious and attractive attitudes there is. I suggest you study it, practice it and embody it as much as possible.

Attitude Transformation Opportunity - Go to your *Get Attitude Playbook* and answer these questions.

- When are two times humility has paid big dividends for me?
- Who is the most humble person I know?
- After interviewing him/her, what are three things I learned?
- Next, list one or two people I can bow to, in honor, and greet them with the "Namaste" gesture and record what happens.
- Lastly, record the next time I achieve greatness and how I became consciously more humble in the experience.

---

2   "Meaning of Namaste - Yoga Journal." 2014. 6 Jul. 2015 <http://www.yogajournal.com/article/beginners/the-meaning-of-quot-namaste-quot/>

O - Openness!

Open your Mind, your Heart and your Wallet. Being open is one of the key factors to having, and holding on to, a good attitude. Why? Primarily, it allows you to accept most everything as considerable, and it prevents you from having your attitude altered. Some people really believe fate is everything, so when something happens to them, for them, or against them, they simply chalk it up as fate. Instead of whining and complaining about things, they just simply look at it as "fate" or a "setback" or "another person's opinion." Occurrences in the life of an attitude achiever are simply viewed and felt as "life", nothing more, nothing less. Having an open mind is the key to allowing yourself not to be manipulated, leveraged or influenced by others and, most importantly, yourself. If attitude is a thinking person's game, then certainly having an open mind would only make sense.

Another way of looking at is to become more accepting of other's habits, thoughts, viewpoints and behaviors. This is what having an open heart means. This is where feeling comes into attitude as described earlier. Is there really any reason to hate or project hate on to another person, situation or occurrence? How does that benefit you? Having an open heart allows you to feel for the other person no matter how long they try and mess up your attitude. It allows you to empathize, not agree or support or endorse, just to simply and easily empathize. Empathy, the ability to understand and share the feelings of another, is the key to success in most business relationships.

Lastly, investing in yourself maybe the hardest thing to do; however, it is the most profitable investment you'll ever make. Who else is going to do it? Who else would you truly expect to do it? If you do not believe you are the best investment for you, why would anyone else? In the words of the great Jim Rohn, "In order for things to change, YOU must change." In order to do that, it will require an investment in time, energy, belief, and money. Open your wallet, you are worth it!

Attitude Transformation Opportunity - Go to your *Get Attitude Playbook* and write these three lists:

- I will open my mind in the following three areas. I will research and understand the issues, people, and philosophies of others and write down what I could potentially gain from an open mind.
- I will open my heart to the three following organizations, people, and groups in order to connect, increase empathy, and understand their perspectives and philosophies.
- I will open my wallet and invest in myself in these three different ways. (personal development seminars, weight watchers, a gym membership, etc…)

Wow, we've made it through more than half of the Alphabet Attitude Challenges! I hope you have been taking advantage of the Attitude Transformation Opportunities. With this tool, you have begun to transform your attitude into what I call an Amazing Attitude.

If you haven't already, download your
Get Attitude Playbook now at
www.abcsofattitude.com
and begin your attitude transformation!

Chapter 7

Attitude for Business

P - Position Yourself for Greatness!

Have you ever thought about who, where, and with whom you want to be within 5-10-20 years? Positioning and proximity are powerful influences of your attitude. Who you hang around does matter. Where you hang around does matter. Putting yourself in the right proximity to those who are like-minded with similar goals and aspirations will enhance and energize your attitude. Certainly you have heard, "Birds of a feather flock together"; well it is true, but why do they? It is amazing to me that some people are trapped hanging around other people in other places that they really do not want to be in. They are trapped, their courage shot, their drive gone because the unmotivated, judgmental, bad attitudes weigh on their conscious mind and emotions and bury the light and hope of their thinking and their positive attitude.

When you position yourself for greatness, you have clarity, certainty and a boldness to declare this is who I am and this is what I am about. You will begin to see avenues where you can position yourself and your message in front of those that can help you, encourage you, invest in you and soar with you. Positioning is one of the most powerful success lessons I have learned. I suggest you find a mentor, someone who is doing what you wish you could be doing in the future. Take note of how they have positioned themselves and take note of their proximity, their physical location, where do they hang out, where are they seen, and what they are surrounded by.

Attitude Transformation Opportunity - Go to your *Get Attitude Playbook* and discover and work on these questions:

- How am I positioned for success currently?
- Who is positioned better than me currently?
- What is my positioning statement? (mine: to change the world one attitude at a time)
- What is my proximity to greatness?
- Where do I want to show up in the world?
- How do I want to be viewed by the world?

Think big, don't hold back, and position yourself in your mind and in the Playbook first for greatness. When you are clear, your attitude will rise and inflate, and so will your lifestyle.

Q - Quick to Serve, Commit and Connect!

I believe that the world has changed and that people's attention spans, patience and expectations have all changed with it. If you are not at least open to the idea of speeding up your game and your life, then you most certainly will be left behind. I certainly understand that this concept will not fit the lifestyles of many. However, those who are happy with complacency, the same old day in day out, and being comfortable in their ways probably did not pick up this book anyway. There are people in life, even in your life, that watch the world pass them by. They are slow to serve, slow to commit and slow to connect, this renders them the antithesis of what Attitude is all about. NOT contagious and NOT attractive to those who have the ability to improve and/or change their lives for the better.

I once heard a saying, "You are either on the bus or under the bus." I believe this to be true; people with Amazing Attitudes and those who embody the secrets in this book will be driving the bus! I've never been one to "ride"; I've always been one to "drive." My guess is that you are too. Certainly, there are times when being a passenger on the bus is acceptable and productive, but my guess is your nature is that of a person who wants to dictate tempo and dominate your own life. This is done through the ability to be quick and swift when it comes to responding to others, decision making, and building rapport with others. I have always believed that the reason I was so successful in sales was my ability to reduce everybody's time investment before a decision was made. How much time does it take for you to make a sale? Time is the only asset distributed equally in the market place. Those who dominate are the ones that are quick, professional and experts in their field. The dominant ones can serve their communities to a higher level, get connections from their clients quicker, thus receiving more commitments and doing more business.

Attitude Transformation Opportunity - Go to your *Get Attitude Playbook* and write down the answers to these questions:

- How long does it take me to respond to other people who I serve?
- How important is it to me that others respond to me quickly? Why is that important? What is my expectation?
- What are five "attitudes" I can develop in order to be a swifter or quicker person in my personal, professional and health life? (Start your answers with…I will dedicate myself to thinking…).

R - Reality Matters!

What is your reality when it comes to your attitude? By now, I hope it has improved and you have discovered some things about yourself and your attitude. Here is a very simple exercise about reality. Try this: take all your clothes off, get in front of a full length mirror, and start jumping up and down. If you want a reality check on the level of your physical condition, this would be the way to get it.

Unfortunately, when we look at all areas of our lives, we don't have a mirror to just hold up and look. It is not that obvious. With our finances, it is pretty easy. Look at how much cash and liquid assets you have in the bank, and that pretty much tells the story. If you have no cash, you may need to add up all those credit card statements you receive monthly and add those up. That will tell you where you are; great reality check.

What is the "mirror" we can use when it comes to our attitude though? What is the reality check when it comes to analyzing your own attitude? Well, certainly there are attitude quizzes and tests you can take; I like the one in Jeffrey Gitomer's *Little Gold Book of Yes! Attitude*. In my opinion, if you answer these three questions daily, you can get a reality check on you attitude very quickly. Record your answers and see how you do.

1. Did everyone I meet leave our experience better off after I left?
2. Did every challenge I faced get addressed and acted upon?
3. In the words of the great Coach Jim Valvano, and his definition of a great day, "Did I laugh, did I think, and did I have my emotions moved to tears today?"

You work on those three questions and I guarantee you, your attitude reality will become clear.

Attitude Transformation Opportunity - Go to your *Get Attitude Playbook* and write down your vision for your new reality.

Include the three questions above on how you will approach and engage everyone you meet, how you will approach and engage challenges you get throughout the day, and lastly, how you can attempt to do all three things that Coach Valvano said were necessary to have a good day.

S - See Things Better than They Are!

This is certainly not a natural thing to do and may be next to impossible for some people to do. Many of us default to actually seeing things worse than they are. Very few of us have the ability to see things as they actually are. Even fewer have the ability to see things better than they are. People with amazing attitudes have practiced and mastered this technique. Some of us were just born with it, most of us not. We need to build that muscle of seeing things better than they are. That will take conscious thought and may take you actually stopping and consciously asking, "What is the good in this?", "How can this help me grow?", "What positive explanation can there be on why this is happening?", "If I see this as better than it is, what does that look like?"

In a nutshell, most people will say this is just like seeing the glass half empty or half full. No, it is seeing the glass full all the time. If you want to be a person who is considered attractive and contagious, develop this skill and process where seeing the glass "full" is just a simple default for where your mind and attitude go in any situation. Stop seeing things as "obstacles", just see them as inconveniences; stop letting rude people upset you, instead, become fascinated with them and see them as people who can develop you positive thinking "glass is full" muscle. You get the picture right?

Attitude Transformation Opportunity - Go to your *Get Attitude Playbook* and write down the three things in your life that you will choose to see as better than they are.

- Write down the benefits to you that will occur by seeing them that way. This may be a relationship, a job, or a perception about yourself or others.

Chapter 8

Attitude of Gratitude

T - Thank You!

This sure is a simple one. Have you ever written a Thank You note and felt worse after you sent it? Have you ever received a Thank You note and felt worse after you read it? I would say it is quite the contrary! We know, and have been told thousands of times, how important it is to say Thank You. Unfortunately, most of us just don't seem to say it or (definitely) write it enough to those people who deserve it. When was the last time you wrote a Thank You note to your spouse, children, or loved one? You might want to try it; the results are usually worth the two minutes of effort it takes. The bigger question is why don't we write Thank you notes when we all know we should? If you have ever started the practice of doing so, was it so hard? Wasn't it certainly well received and paid dividends for your relationship? Yet, we still make excuses like… I can't find the time, my printing is bad, I forgot. You know them all. What are you telling yourself when it comes to writing Thank You notes, or even picking up the phone and making a thank you call?

The answer to the question on why we don't express our thankfulness to others is quite simple. It is our Attitude about sending the card…It is that we have not dedicated ourselves to a way of thinking that makes us feel that this practice must be done. We don't feel uncomfortable enough NOT sending the note because we fail so often to even send them. Rephrased, we are so comfortable not sending them, so there is no pain associated with our lack of initiative to thank those who deserve to be thanked. Try this, write Thank you notes every day for thirty straight days, then stop writing them for thirty days. I can assure you after you have written them for 30 days, you will feel totally uncomfortable not writing them. You will finally feel the emptiness, lack of gratitude and disconnection with those you know who should receive the simple kindness of a note. Thank you notes are one of the most underutilized business secrets in America. Those who make it a practice tend to have higher incomes, successes and most definitely Amazing Attitudes.

Attitude Transformation Opportunity - Go to your *Get Attitude Playbook* and keep a Thank You count.

- How many times a day are you saying and writing Thank You? Keep a record for a week and you will see the higher your score the higher the Attitude.
- List 25 people who should receive a Thank You note from you

Then, I suggest you get busy writing, one per day will do!

U - Uplift!

Perhaps the greatest gift of all that people with Amazing Attitudes have is the ability to uplift. Every person, team, business, event, or occurrence all have the potential to be raised to the next level. Those who read this book and study attitude have the ability to feel the exhilaration of making this happen with all the previous mentioned circumstances. For additional tools and examples, I recommend reading *Pushing Up People* by Art Williams. You bring so much to your business, your life, and the world when you take time to value and encourage others.

Not only is it great to be the one who is uplifting others, but people with Amazing Attitudes allow themselves to be uplifted as well. This too is just as important a gift as being the one who uplifts. You can't grow if you are not open to being uplifted. Do you look around your life or your day with the intent or purpose of finding situations to lift others up? Most people do not wake up and say, "Who can I uplift today?" It is not common, but if practiced will make you stand out big time. Talk about being attractive and contagious; be the one who dares to pull others up from their circumstance, pull people through to their goals and pull people out of their negative thinking and mindset.

One of my favorite saying about sales and leadership Tom Hopkins is, "We don't push people, we pull people." The concept of pull vs. push is a great vehicle to uplift those around you. Pull people with your questions, your encouragement and most of all your example.

Attitude Transformation Opportunity - Go to your *Get Attitude Playbook* and identify three people, groups, events or occurrences that are going to get uplifted the next time they encounter you.

What are you going to be, do and say when these opportunities arise?

V - Vitality!

When you see people with Amazing Attitudes, the one thing you see and feel around them is this incomparable aura. They have incredible energy which almost oozes out of them when they speak and look into your eyes. Their ability to connect with you is easy and alluring. They look as though they possess an exuberant physical strength and mental vigor. I call this an "Attitude Secret Sauce." That secret sauce is called vitality- the state of being strong and active.

Vitality has many different definitions, like the one listed above. However, when vitality and attitude are mentioned in the same arena, I think the definition of vitality that fits best is the capacity for survival or for the continuation of a meaningful or purposeful existence. Strength, energy, capacity and the power to grow are great synonyms for what we speak of when we talk about vitality.

Vitality, when it comes to attitude, is everything. Once you have developed your attitude, you need to continue to feed it, maintain it and reinforce it. You would do this by working on it every day. Just as a person may work out at the gym every day and eat right to attain their physical and mental vitality, you must everyday (if only for three minutes) daily work on you attitude vitality achievement. Your attitude needs to possess exuberant strength, mental vigor, a capacity for survival, an intent purposeful existence and the attitude power to grow. Attitude vitality is the culmination of this study. It makes your attitude unshakable, powerful and bullet proof.

Attitude Transformation Opportunity - Go to your *Get Attitude Playbook* and write what you will look like, feel like, and how you will present yourself when your attitude vitality is instilled in your mind.

W - Wholeheartedness!

What a great way to dedicate yourself; to be fully or completely sincere, enthusiastic, energetic and hearty. Be earnest in your endeavors. What if you approached life in this manner, what if you approached your attitude in this manner?

As Jim Rohn once said, "Wherever you are, be there." This is not easy to do. Especially with technology today, alerts, calls, dings from emails. It is an ever increasing epidemic that I see two people sitting sharing a lunch table and both are totally engrossed in their technology. What is even worse is when I see a couple and one of them is nose down in the phone, even worse than that, a parent literally ignoring their child and working on their cell phone. Some people make the effort to set the time, very few make the effort to spend the time, completely, wholeheartedly with the person in front of them.

What does half-hearted attention get you? Don't those who you love and serve deserve the total you? Half-hearted attention gets you half the results, half the bonding, half the joy of wholehearted attention, a whole hearted attitude.

If you think Thank You notes are tough, try this one on for size. Just imagine how your life and relationships would change if you dedicated yourself to writing Thank You notes daily. Imagine actually putting away your cell phone while you are in a face to face meeting with friends, family or business associates. You engage in these two practices, I believe you'll get attitude and your income will double.

Attitude Transformation Opportunity - Go to your *Get Attitude Playbook* and list the two activities and the two people you are going to commit to give a wholehearted attitude to. Write down three ways you will demonstrate how this will happen. I promise you those four recipients will be thankful and their attitudes will improve right along with yours.

Chapter 9

Attitude Refreshers

X - XOXO - HUGS and KISSES!

I understand some people just are not the warm and fuzzy type. It freaks them out to give or receive hugs and kisses. I guess that begs the question, why? Which begs the question, "Are people with more positive attitudes more comfortable with hugs and kisses?" In my experience, YES! Think about people who are angry, hateful, upset, or stressed out; the last thing they want is someone coming up and smiling, opening their arms and saying, "Bring it in for a big hug!" It is quite the opposite; they are closed, often with arms crossed hugging themselves. They struggle to move beyond a negative attitude and miss out on making meaningful connections.

I find people who are happy, loving and possessing many of the previously mentioned attitudes are more than happy to give and receive a hug. They see and feel the joy of another's energy. I've never seen two people give a hug when one has a bad attitude; it just doesn't happen. Through out my lifetime, I have had the ability to connect instantly with other huggers and we just hug from the very first meeting. I know this sounds impossible to some people, but this phenomena does exist. The Instant Hugging Syndrome!

Can you have a good attitude without being a hugger? Well, I guess so, but I would encourage you to investigate and find out why you are so against a hug. Why does a hug make you feel so uncomfortable? There are people where this practice is going to be as hard as writing that Thank You note or putting down that cell phone in order to give the wholehearted attitude people are attracted to and that creates contagious energy.

Attitude Transformation Opportunity - Take out your *Get Attitude Playbook* and write down the reasons you love to hug and be hugged.

- Then write down the circumstances in which you do not like to be hugged.
- Go and figure a way to be so positive, happy and loving that three hugs a day become inevitable in your life.
- Record the three people who gave you those hugs when you normally wouldn't receive them. Record how it felt.
- Then send them a Thank You note!

Y - Yummy!

The principle of yummy is a great attitude booster! When is the last time you bit into something so scrumptious and good that it just changed your attitude? I'm sure there are foods and smells so divine and good that they just lift your attitude right to the sky! What if you could just take a bite all day and never be in a poor attitude? Well, some people do that, but that causes them to actually become addicted to it which has obvious negative consequences. Physical addiction and attitude addiction together can be a costly experiment. Food, alcohol, and drugs are all common attitude boosters that people use too much in order to get their attitude right. The principle of yummy involves you understanding the anticipation and satisfaction of whatever stimulus is in front of you. Instead of food, alcohol or drugs, I challenge you to look at problems, occurrences, people and tasks as yummy, just like those vices listed above. Just think how your life can change when you look at your next problem and say, "Man, what a YUMMY problem!" It will give you a different way of looking and thinking about that problem and you solution will be much more proactive positive and allow you to eat it up!

Attitude Transformation Opportunity - Take out your *Get Attitude Playbook* and write down a YUMMY problem that you are dealing with right now.

How can I face this problem with anticipation?

Z - Zamboni!

Yes, you have the ability to be a Zamboni each and every day you wake up! A Zamboni is the machine that comes out at hockey games after every period to "clear" the ice. If you have ever seen one perform, it is amazing! I love the sport of hockey; it is played on ice by players who all wear ice skates. There are 12 people on the ice at a time for a 20 minute period. Every time each player moves, he/she leaves an impression on the ice; it marks where they have been. It marks, by the depth of its cut, the ferocity of their encounter. At times, there are chunks taken out of the ice when two players collide. All that activity, interaction, passion, good or bad, has in some way been marked on that ice by the skates of those players. There are very few patches of ice that have not been touched. For the most part, however, the ice surface that has been played on is marked up; it tells a story. At the end of each period, the Zamboni comes out and wipes clear all marks, fills all divots and crevices, and we begin a new period with a new slate of ice.

You are the Zamboni of your attitude. You have the control, the machine, the technology to wipe away all the marks of you and your fellow players as it pertains to attitude. We are all in this game together. We all play on the same surface- some better than others. We all leave our marks on the ice of life and time. I encourage you to daily clean and clear those markings and start fresh with a clear, crisp, clean slab of "ice" and attitude. If you can visualize what a hockey rink looks like after the Zamboni does its thing, you will get the picture. The rink is always at its peak when it is clean. There is no real benefit to studying the marks of the last period. For ultimate attitude performance, living in the last period will only slow you down. Be bold, be clear, be clean, and clean up your attitude. You are the Zamboni, and nothing will prevent you from a new beginning, just like the teams at the beginning of a new period!

Failure and mistakes are a big part of sports, sales, and life. Those who can adopt this philosophy will endure and productively smash failure and mistakes -- and leave regret and guilt in the ice. You will find yourself changing your life and the lives of others around you with your new philosophy.

Attitude Transformation Opportunity - Go to your *Get Attitude Playbook* and write down the marks and divots of your "iced" attitude. It is time to acknowledge the attitude choices of the past and then wipe them away. List three attitudes in your past that need to get cleaned and wiped away. Now is the time to start fresh with an Amazing Attitude!

At the end of each Alphabet Attitude Challenge, you were presented with an Attitude Transformation Opportunity. You've been asked to take out your *Get Attitude Playbook* and write down your responses to thought provoking questions. With this tool, you began to transform your attitude into what I call an Amazing Attitude.

If you haven't already, download your *Get Attitude Playbook* now at <u>www.abcsofattitude.com</u> and begin your attitude transformation!

Part Three

Make a Difference with Your New Attitude!

GOALS

Continue your Attitude transformation by:

- Learning The Attitude Engagement Formula!
- Recognizing how Attitude Influences Sales!
- Continuing to be Inspired to Get Attitude!

Chapter 10

How You Show Up Matters

"I've learned that people will forget what you said, people will forget what you did, but people will never forget how you made them feel."

\- Maya Angelou

It is important to understand that a first impression is not just about how you are "seen." It is about how you create an impact on the person in front of you. It is about how you make someone else feel; how they feel about themselves and feel about you. It is about what goes on not only in their heart (feeling), but what also goes on in their head. How are you impacting their thinking? Yes, it is all about how they think about you and how they feel about you. A first impression also encompasses how you make someone think and feel about themselves.

I've always believed the popular saying, "You never get a second chance to make a first impression." When creating a first impression, it is important to ask yourself, "How am I showing up?"

That is why I'd like for you to consider the philosophy "**HOW you show up matters**." Why? I don't believe the masses study **HOW**

TO SHOW UP. I think they give it a thought, show up the way they always do, and get the results they always get.

A first impression is based on the following:

1. A gut feeling, way down deep
2. A judgement, fair or not, by another party (thinking)
3. An instinct (kind of like cats and dogs)

And results in:

1. The decision to do business or not
2. The calculation to enter a relationship or not
3. The beginning of a chain of events that could change your life

If you think about, and really review, these results of a first impression, one undoubtedly can understand that how we show up matters. How we show up may actually be the most important differentiator in human relationships today. Are there people in your life that just plain do not know how to show up? Oftentimes, teenagers and young adults do not understand how to show up. Do you remember being careless about how you showed up when you were younger? Some of us were never taught the basics of making a good impression or the value of showing up and giving your all.

Think just for a second about how you are showing up in the world and how you have shown up throughout the past month, year or decade to people. Think about how others have shown up for you and how instantly you get a gut feeling, form a judgement, create an instinct, make a decision, calculate the outcome and either start a chain of events or stop the chain of events from beginning with that person.

I want you to understand How You Show Up is more than just a saying; it needs to be studied, thought about and developed. We have all blown it in how we show up. I've probably made more mistakes than anyone reading this book! Now is your chance to turn the table and begin to show up like you never have before.

**How You Show Up needs to become, yes
you guessed it, an Attitude!**

Introductions and first impressions are made within less than a minute! You know this, but how good are you at making a good impression? If all you get from this book is how to show up better, it will already be worth it!

Understand there are many ways people teach how to show up. Many experts may disagree with this; however, I believe like-minded people seem to agree and get along better. I realize there is no rule, but if you try this, my hunch is your results will improve.

Let me give you my **Attitude Engagement Formula** for showing up that will change your life forever.

1. **Look Good Feel Good** - The way you look matters, period. People judge you on your looks instantly, especially in a professional setting. I believe you can never over dress. I know of specific instances when showing up underdressed cost people opportunities to advance relationships, photograph their associations and limited their access to important people or venues. Has this ever happened to you? Feeling good is about your energy is transferrable; people can feel it through your handshake, see it through your smile and hear it in your voice.

2. **Have Passion and Emotion** - Although there are people who are turned off by excited, passionate people, those

who have influence, attraction and a positive attitude treasure the interaction with people who possess these two great traits, especially if they recognize it right up front.

3. **SMILE always through the first physical contact** - Do you really think people are more attracted to people who don't smile? Who would you rather meet, a smiling stranger or a stranger with no emotion on their face, or even worse a frown?

4. **Drill them with EYE CONTACT, look through them into their soul** - Some people feel intimidated by this, but this is about showing up as confident, assertive and fearless. In a business situation especially, the recipient who stares back can most likely influence your future for the positive. If you look away or down, that person may not think you have the MOXY to produce for them.

5. **EMPATHIZE with how they are feeling in the moment** - This is learned, felt and developed. If your skill is poor at this, you need to meet more people. The best way to do this is to listen (which my good friend John Hannon taught me is defined as "wanting to hear"), ask them to explain further, then repeat their thoughts and words. Finally, ask them afterward if they feel like you understand their feelings correctly. You may say something like, "Do I seem to understand what you are saying or feeling correctly?"

6. **Ask them QUESTIONS about them** - This is fairly obvious, the best way to do this is to first ask yourself, "what questions would I want people to ask me about myself?" I love this technique. Write them down, practice, drill, and rehearse, and you will see people are fascinated with your inquiry on their favorite subject - THEM.

7. **LISTEN to their answers** - I know it's hard, but really listen. Stop formulating what you want to say while they are sharing. This is one of the biggest mistakes I see

people make. Although we assume one person talks and the other listens, this is often not the case. Many books, such as The Lost Art of Listening, have been been written about this technique. Ask more questions about what they think and feel - The technique is simple, just take the time to ask, "Tell me why you think that way or tell me why you feel that way?"

8. **If they ask you a question, ANSWER DIRECTLY, and with certainty** - The best way to do this is talk about things you have actually done. If they want to know more, they will ask you. Too many people talk about what they are going to do, or what they should do. People who discuss and communicate about accomplishments never completed, thoughts never acted on and actions never taken only come off as pretenders, not as contenders.

9. **TELL them, "I really love your ATTITUDE!"** - Yes, really do it! People love compliments, and this one shows that you have been paying attention and care about attitude.

10. **Then ASK, "How did you GET YOURS?"** - Yes, do this too! Do you have the guts?

You do this and the world will see that you are showing up like never before!

Note: This formula is based on meeting someone spontaneously. If you have the opportunity to research someone prior to the meeting, then you are armed with even more ammunition to show up better than anyone else.

TRUTH: 99% of people are more interested in themselves, their thoughts and their feelings more than anyone else. Including you!

If they are not showing up right, perhaps you will refer them to this book and suggest they to go to www.universityofattitude.com

Let's face it, we can all recall that one person who we met that has had a major influence over our life, and it all began with how you showed up to them and how they showed up to you. This could have been:

- Your best friend
- A mentor
- A future spouse
- A great love
- A business partner
- A new boss

The painful circumstance to me is when I reflect on all my missed opportunities because of how I showed up. Since this is a book about attitude, mostly positive attitude, you need to come to terms with those memories, and move on and show up like you never have before.

ATTITUDE REALIZATION: When you have to meet or call on someone new, understand they could be the missing KEY to the rest of your life.

When I train salespeople on customer service and "showing up" (which is exactly what customer service is), I always tell them to think about how they treat a "normal joe" walking through the door and how they would react and "show up" if it were Brad Pitt, Angelina Jolie and for those readers who hate people, what if it were a dog! It is crazy to watch people transform when they actually think about how they would treat a celebrity as opposed to a "normal customer."

**If you develop the Attitude of Celebrity and
start treating everyone like they are a celebrity,
you will see your attitude, your mood, your
fun and your happiness increase.**

Try it for a day. Pick the celebrity you would most like to meet and treat everyone you see today as that person, or for you animal lovers, that puppy!

How you are showing up is a direct reflection on how your life is going. I believe there is proportionality to that equation. Everyone is trying to find the ultimate differentiator.

Is it adding value, creating an experience, differentiation, being a game changer, or celebrity?

> I believe the ultimate differentiator is ATTITUDE.
> Let's continue learning how to have
> an Amazing Attitude!

What is your attitude about How You Show Up?

Attitude Transformation Opportunity - Go to your *Get Attitude Playbook* and list the three times you showed up and killed it and the three times you showed up and it killed you. This might be painful, but "no pain, no gain!"

Chapter 11

Attitude and Sales

"Most people buy not because they believe,
but because the sales person believes."
- Ben Feldman

People don't sell because you tell them to...
They sell because they believe in something.
EMPOWER PEOPLE.

I have had a long career in sales. I have sold, managed those who sold and trained those who sold. People who are really good at sales, no matter what they are selling, have one common core quality, it is called BELIEF! This is not a sales training book, but this is a book about your attitude; what are you believing about your attitude? Sales isn't just about product sales, there is sales in religion, medicine, politics; you name it, sales is everywhere. The difference makers and the difference leaders are those who can effectively communicate to their audience what their belief is and why their belief will benefit those who listen. So, what are you selling? If you really take a look at your business or life, you are selling something and what you're selling is a belief in something. Your attitude will affect your intensity regarding that belief.

The better the attitude, the more the belief, the more the sales, the more the success. The worse the attitude, the weaker the belief, the weaker the sales, the less the success. It is quite simple.

Attitude Transformation Opportunity - Go to your *Get Attitude Playbook*, ask yourself these questions and write down your responses.

- What am I selling?
- What is my attitude toward what I am selling?
- If I believe in what I am selling, how or what must my improved attitude be in order to create more attraction around my sale?

Remember you may not be selling a product. You may simply be selling a lifestyle, such as "stay at home mom." The public has all kinds of attitudes on "stay at home parenting." All that matters is what you believe, what your attitude is toward it, and how it aligns with your lifestyle and presentation to the world. Your belief will attract and be contagious just like your attitude. They are and need to be in alignment in order for you to empower others. Empowering others can, in fact, change the world and most importantly your world!

The Attitude of Hurry: CUSTOMERS ARE INTERESTED IN A SHORT EASY SALES CYCLE

The secret to market dominance is your ability to first meet a customer and get them to trust you enough to do business in the shortest amount of time possible. I call this the Attitude of Hurry.

People don't like to be hurried or rushed and great salespeople present an environment or attitude where the customer believes

they are benefitting by making quick decisions and appreciate salespeople who save their most precious resource TIME.

How does that happen? It is called Expertise. The public knows if you are an expert or not. If you look at the top three salespeople in any organization, those people all have one thing in common, they do transactions in less time than their other sales counterparts. Real experts are rewarded by pay, commissions and cash. Their 1099 is a reflection of their expertise. How can a person sell 100 houses in a year while the fellow sitting next to him only sold 12? One answer is that instead of spending 20 hours with a client, the expert may only be spending two.

Here is the point, no one has time anymore. Those of us who don't use the people that are the experts, the best in the business, who are easy to do business with and cut through the waste and get to the point, are missing out on business.

As a customer, the last thing I want to do is deal with a salesperson who has the attitude that we can take as long as needed and has no urgency. When there is no urgency in the sales process, this indicates problems due to the salesperson's lack of knowledge and efficiency.

I had a sales rep at one time in my life named Julie Catton; she was smart enough to ask me how I want to be handled as her customer. I told her simply to answer me in one of two ways when I had a request. Those two statements were:

1. We will get on that right away.
2. You will see immediate results.

How easy is that? Wouldn't you want to be handled in this manner as a customer?

I have always admired her ability to deliver what I asked her to do. She said it with a smile; even though she may not have agreed, she always delivered based on those two elements. That answer is all about attitude. That answer made her attractive to me and contagious, because when I dealt with other reps in her profession and they did not answer me that way, then I would crave her service!

Either you are good enough or you are not. You don't decide, the customer does. In this instance, I decided she was going be my rep until she left the business.

Attitude Transformation Opportunity - Go to your *Get Attitude Playbook* and answer these questions.

- How easy are you to do business with?
- Are you **the** expert in your field?
- Have you interviewed the three people in your market who are better than you and noticed a difference?

If you take the time to do this, you will accelerate your success.

Lessons From the 4th Quarter

As a coach and businessman, I love making connections between what works in the field and what works in the office and in life. In football, why does everyone put so much emphasis on the final quarter? The answer is obvious: time is running out. A great motivator in life, and in sales, is called URGENCY. Urgency is created day by day -- or minute by minute as the fourth quarter ticks away. Are you prepared? Here are your fourth quarter keys for success:

1. **Get stronger through the contest**. Condition your mind and body in a way where you have the strength to exceed

your effort from the previous quarters. For you, these quarters may be minutes, hours, days, or week. No matter what the timeline, keep pushing yourself. See yourself as never tiring, always positive, and as mentally tough as anyone you meet. Focus on your strength, own your strength, and give it away to no one. Expect yourself to be the strongest player at the end of a challenge, those who finish strong expect it, create the outcome and demand increased will through the end not till the end.

2. **Don't be afraid to win the game**. We condition our players and salespeople to expect to win the game and to make the big play. Fourth-quarter victories are found deep down in the hearts of players who relish in the opportunity to exceed their beliefs, their plans, and go after the moment right away with no concern of failure.

3. **Always do more for others than for yourself.** We know through the study of human behavior that our players and salespeople will always commit and perform more for others than just for themselves. Win the game for your team.

4. **Train and prepare for your fourth quarter well before it hits.** Dominate by improving your performance one day at a time. Don't focus on your next play, focus on your next day. A powerful exercise is to divide whatever time you have left in this year into four segments and make the last segment of your year your fourth quarter. Most importantly, have the Amazing Attitude it takes to thrive in your fourth quarter no matter how long it is.

Attitude Transformation Opportunity - Go to your *Get Attitude Playbook* and identify what you need to accomplish in your fourth quarter.

Exponential Customer Attraction: Social Media and You

It is a new world. Marketing is FREE! Publicity is FREE! You can create your own channel on YouTube if you want. Here is the point, you are either actively participating in social media or you are not. Chances are, the reason you are or are not is based on your attitude about the validity of social media, the privacy of social media or the benefits of social media.

Many of you see no value at all in social media. I am not here to judge one way or the other. I don't care if you like it or don't like it. I will tell you that those who have an open attitude about it are enjoying more connection, more conversation and more engagement than ever before, especially those who are sixty years old and above.

It amazes me the countless people I talk to who are over sixty who have found a way to text or Facebook. They are more engaged and connected with their family, from their kids to their grandkids. There are a lot of attitudes around social media, most of them are negative by the "non-users" because they are not engaged. They are getting shut out and it is only going to increase. People communicate differently today.

Self-improvement is about being a great communicator. Those of you who have taken a hold of this new medium are getting it slowly and surely, but this is a tidal wave that is not turning back. I encourage you to open your mind, heart and attitude to engaging with the world, or even just your families, a little more through the gift of social media.

You can make money on social media by learning Business Social Media strategies. All you have to do is watch the nightly news, morning talk shows, the Fortune 500 companies or the best local marketers in your area and you will see them posting, engaging with their communities and making big money.

This is not a book about how to make money on social media. This is a book to help you open your mind to the benefits, both personally and professionally, in social media and investigate if you want to ride that wave or not.

Attitude Transformation Opportunity - Go to your *Get Attitude Playbook* and answer these questions.

- What are my thoughts/attitudes about social media?
- Can I think of a way that social media can help me form and build connections in my business and personal life?

If you were your own customer, would you hire you?

One of the expectations I set for myself as a business person was the "I am my own customer" expectation. Ultimately, in any adventure, venture or business you undertake, aren't you ultimately the customer you must please?

I am a very demanding customer; I consider that a gift. My attitude when it comes to service is rarely matched. My intensity on customer experience and communication is a driving force that burns in me, and when I don't receive it or deliver it, it affects my attitude. It is one of the biggest challenges high producers face when it comes to attitude.

How do we turn it off? How do we disengage from a business we love so much that fulfills our most every emotional need? The answer: you've got to work at it. Just like you've got to work at your attitude. Go back to the RID OF formula and continue to adjust, continue to take more halftime breaks and plan, analyze and adjust each day to how your game is going.

It just amazes me that people do not perform as they expect others to perform for them. Simple question, are you one of those people? This is not an easy answer to get to, but the next time you go to dinner and get annoyed with a server who is doing ten tables at a time, ask yourself if you would be juggling what they are in the same manner? Do I juggle everything in my day, my business day, in the same manner? Do I have grace? Do I make everyone feel important even though I have no time? Do I do the little things that show I am on top of my game, or do I ignore them, pass them off as unimportant and not deliver to the level I know I can? What is your attitude when receiving and giving service?

Attitude Transformation Opportunity - Go to your *Get Attitude Playbook* and complete the following sentences.

- When I receive service, I tend to be…
- When I give service, I tend to be…

Chapter 12

Amazing Attitude Inspiration

Over the years I have copied down some of the most powerful quotes about attitude that I have heard. I hope the following will help you further your mind, your thoughts and your understanding of attitude. Perhaps, a few of these questions, and there are many, will help you in your search for attitude adjustment. I credit many of my attitude mentors in this section and I hope you purchase their information as you continue your attitude study.

After each inspirational quote, you will be presented with Attitude Transformation Opportunities. You'll be asked to take out your *Get Attitude Playbook* and write down your responses to thought provoking questions. With this tool, you will begin to transform your attitude into what I call an Amazing Attitude.

Download your *Get Attitude Playbook*
now at <u>www.abcsofattitude.com</u>
and begin your attitude transformation!

"You can't get out of life alive."
- Les Brown

One of my favorite mentors! When I heard this, as obvious as it seems, so many of us think our ultimate demise will never come.

Not that we should dwell on our end, but keeping your mortality awake in your mind tends to drive your attitude to action and accomplishment. What do you want to have accomplished when your death comes? We do not know the day, the time or the hour, so I chase that end with passion, with clarity, and with empathy for others. Do you?

Attitude Transformation Opportunity - Do you think about what you want it to say on your gravestone? Go to your *Get Attitude Playbook* and write about how you want to be remembered.

> *"If you want to be remembered tomorrow,*
> *do something great today."*
> - Martin Rooney

Think about it. Do you really get up every day and believe you are going to do something that is great? My guess is very few people do. Think about this, what if you did? Just imagine if you consciously said to yourself when your eyes first open, "I am going to do something great today!" You can only imagine what the majority of people say and think to themselves the very first thing in the morning; my guess is it is not about changing the world, doing greatness or impacting the emotions of another person they may meet in a positive sense. You can make history everyday. The question is, do you? Most people only make history once a year, maybe not even that. Raise your expectations; you are perhaps as great as you think you are. If you don't believe it, no one else will either!

Attitude Transformation Opportunity - Start every day saying, "I am going to do something great today!" Go to your *Get Attitude Playbook* and write down three ways that you are going to make history!

> *"When you're tired, sore, and can't do more,*
> *that's the time to do more."*
> - Tim Grover

If you get hurt, your opportunity to play lessens. Ask yourself the question, "Am I really hurt?"

This question is harsh, but it is a reality. It certainly is a reality in the culture I've been in for twenty five years of coaching. How much or how little does your physical state affect your decision to get out of bed and get to work? More importantly, how does it affect your ability/desire to Get Attitude? Have you caved or taken off when you really did not need to? Have you let someone you love do the same because it hurts you to watch them endure some pain? **Is it not true that the ability to witness a loved one's pain is the ultimate sign of love? Provided you are confident, after the test, they come out for the better on the other side.**

> "Reject your sense of injury and
> the injury itself disappears."
> - Marcus Aurelius, *Meditations*

The reality is everyday you take off is a day a competitor, friendly or not, gains on you. I am not advocating never taking a day off, but the truth of achievement often finds itself in the balance or imbalance of how you are spending your time. If you have an attitude about time off that is more accepting than those who are pursuing greatness, you are going to be left behind.

I have never considered myself lazy, I have always considered myself as a goal directed purposeful person. Someone who had an innate sense if my effort was lacking. Many people do not have this. It needs to be learned, cultivated and experienced. The best way to do this is through coaching and mentoring. Whether in a sport, in a business or in a relationship, the battle of time in all these areas conflicts. You may not be taking time off in your business, but you may be taking time off in your relationships, and that can also cost you. Taking time off means not dealing with or engaging with the attitudes necessary to move you and the ones you love forward.

There is always someone out there watching you, observing your work habits, and planning how to surpass you. I'm not saying this to make you paranoid, but understand that they are there.

You may not care, but someday you will, when you stand up and say, "Where did it all go?"

Many of us act like we are hurt, believe we are hurt, whether it is physical, mental or emotional, but understand this, the market doesn't care, a lot of times your boss doesn't care, and if you are a habitual injured player, soon enough your friends and family won't care.

If you truly get hurt, the painful reality is life will go on, competition will continue and you will get trounced.

I believe that having a preventative attitude plan will keep you from being on the injured list. Can your attitude really pull you through the times when you are hurting most? I say definitely! How and why can I say this? For the same reason you can. We have all faced adversity, not just normal adversity, but real big and painful adversity. Adversity so bad that we were hurt, but there was that one thing that kept us going. It was deep in our heart, our mind and our soul. I call this your preventative attitude plan.

Some people had this plan coached into them, some had this practiced into them, some had learned it on their own through personal experience. "I will never give up, I will never give up", and so you did not. By not giving up, you squashed the opportunity for the next in line to feast on your prize. The prize of life.

Being hurt is understandable, not playing hurt is understandable, but understand this: no one is going to "wait" on you to get better, and in some way everyone is replaceable. If you don't believe it, go ahead and tempt fate!

If I focused on other's stories, I am sure I could write a whole new book on this one!

Attitude Transformation Opportunity - Go to your *Get Attitude Playbook* and write down when you benefitted from someone who stayed on the bench and when you got robbed by "not playing."

> *"If it doesn't challenge you, it doesn't change you."*
> - Fred DeVito

I love challenges; they make me rich! Changing your attitude when it comes to challenges is perhaps the most life changing and fun activity you can do! When a challenge comes my way, I like to say, "It is a great day for an upset!" Unfortunately, many people do not want to be challenged. They do not want their ideas challenged, their beliefs challenged, their results challenged, their religion challenged, their relationships challenged, their honesty challenged, their physical condition challenged and most of all, their attitude challenged. I don't care…challenge away because challenges make you rich! They don't just make you monetarily rich, but they make you rich in spirit, compassion, understanding, knowledge, wisdom, and most of all attitude. See, challenges strengthen your attitude. It is a lot like the saying "Iron sharpens iron." If your attitude is never challenged, it can become weak, (unless you are one of the few who go out and work on attitude development everyday) it can become apathetic, you are not forced to defend it, use it, negotiate with it or influence with it. Pain in the ass people are a part of life, their purpose is to help you sharpen and strengthen your attitude so they either quit wanting to hang around you or become influenced enough by your energy that they want to "GET SOME ATTITUDE" like yours! The next challenge you run up against, no matter personal, professional, technological or financial- smile and say, "You are gonna make me rich. Bring it on!" Don't you feel better about all the wonderful challenges you have in your life now?

Attitude Transformation Opportunity - Go to your *Get Attitude Playbook* and write out your five biggest challenges. Then write a Thank You note for each challenge and state why or how this challenge will make you rich.

> *"Inveniam Viam- I shall either find a way or make one."*
> - Seneca, Roman philosopher

I love this quote. I've said this, I have felt this, I have lived this. My guess is you have too! Especially, if you are reading this book. This quote inspires me to think that your destiny is in your control; if you think otherwise, you will be right. I can also assure you that someone else's vision, hopes and dreams for you are not near what they are for yourself. Don't try things someone else's way without careful diagnostics and consideration. Many of us try things someone else's way only to find out their way is the wrong way. Your destiny is yours, no one else's, your thoughts are yours, no one else's, and unfortunately for us, your results are yours, no one else's if you choose to accept this philosophy I've just put forth. I believe it is always best to start or end your challenges by analyzing if you can find a way or make your own way.

Attitude Transformation Opportunity - Go to your *Get Attitude Playbook* and write about a time when someone else's way didn't work for you.

How did you find your own way through that challenge?

"Who are you and what are you about?"
- Coach McGinley

I was asked this question by a fellow coach not just about me as a person, but about us as a team. Who are we and what are we about? This is called Attitude Identity. Unless you really know who you are as a person or a team or a company and it is written down, thought about daily, considered, reconsidered, argued about, your identity will get crushed in competition. Someone else who really knows who they are and what they are about will defeat you. It is called "imposing your will" on your competitor. This is more easily defined in a sports competition where you can physically see one team, or individual, dominating another; however, it is harder to see in the area of attitude and influence. Most people who are at the top of their game, who seem to win most of the time, who are happy, have the answers to these two questions.

Attitude Transformation Opportunity - Go to your *Get Attitude Playbook* and answer those two questions. It may take a few times, but your answer should be no longer than three sentences for each question. Trust me, very few do this, or have ever done this. Take the time for Attitude Identity, and you will see your attitude influence many more people than it does right now.

"Simplicity is the key to brilliance."
- Bruce Lee

SIMPLE IS WORTH MILLIONS

How complicated do you make your day? Your week? Your month? Your year? A decision? Most decisions? Every decision? I've always been fortunate that I am a simple person. Decisions and choices come very easy to me. I drive analytical people crazy and they drive me crazy. I believe simply this, life is about the fundamentals. So are choices, so are decisions, so are relationships. There are only 3-6 fundamentals in every challenge you face. Identify and focus on those 3-6 and move forward; it is simple. When making a decision, identify the the best benefits and the three worst consequences. When working on improving your health, financial freedom, and relationships, focus on simple reminders, such as eat right and exercise, spend less than you make, and lead with love.

Attitude Transformation Opportunity - Go to your *Get Attitude Playbook* and write about an important decision that you need to make.

- For each potential outcome, what are the best three benefits?
- What are the worst three consequences?

> *"Feedback is the breakfast of Champions."*
> - Jack Canfield

I say "Get Some!"

When making changes in life, such as transforming our attitude, it is important to get feedback from others. It can be difficult to identify our own growth and areas of improvement. Sometimes an outside perspective can help you figure out your next step. You are creating your own path, and I don't advise listening to every single opinion. However, find a mentor and be open to their feedback regarding your attitude transformation.

Attitude Transformation Opportunity - Go to your *Get Attitude Playbook* and identify a mentor who can provide meaningful feedback.

- What specific feedback do you need? What questions will you ask?

> *"Commitment is the glue*
> *that bonds you to your goals."*
> - Jill Koenig

Are you going to commit to and achieve your goals? If you have an Amazing Attitude, the answer is - Yes!

"I am not sure…" is an unacceptable answer.

This saying coupled with the words "can't" and "try" make my attitude get a little negative! I should probably work on that! Actually, as an initial reaction, I understand it sometimes…but after a person has thought and studied this book, my hope for them is that these words vacate their vocabulary.

Really, what can you accomplish and achieve by saying these words to other people and, even worse, to yourself? I loved it when the great Tony Robbins demonstrated this point in his seminar when he asked a lady to "*try* to pick up the chair." Of course, she did and picked it up, he said, "No, you picked it up, *try* to pick it up." She looked at him as if he were crazy, she was a bit confused, then she laid her hands on the hair. Tony said, "Ah, ah, ah, don't move it, just try and move it. Then the point set in, trying usually accomplishes nothing. It gets you to a place of immobility, confusion, and inaction. It is a great excuse when you are not doing, people actually will buy into it and accept it. Those of us with an attitude of doing and achieving, simply won't. The same goes for the word can't. Lastly, these are the mantras of the "I'm not sure" crowd. Have you ever asked your kid, "Why did you do that?" and they say, "I am not sure.".... Ugh, not the right answer.

There are reasons people do things and to allow the answer to why someone else or yourself does something to be, "I am not sure" only takes you, and them, off the hook. It creates a lack of accountability.

I suggest you create a little conflict and drill down on why someone else, or yourself, does things that are stupid, reckless and destructive. Don't allow them to say, "I am not sure." I have done this with numerous people and most of the time the answer can be found... "because I was being selfish".

Try this with yourself, your kids, or your friends the next time you hear these words come out of your or their mouth. These sayings are the antithesis to attitude. Ultimately, they amount to "I don't want to be dedicated to thinking" or "I do not want to feel anything beyond complacency."

There are many who focus on what they can and can't do, but that is all they do...focus, dream and think about it. The next step in the process is to understand what you want to do; this involves a little deeper commitment, increased thought, and in most cases, involves a person's Why? Here is the issue. I ask the masses, "Just give me one thing, action or activity where you are committed to what you will be doing." I usually get a blank stare. This is a productive exercise for sure. When setting out to achieve something, the most important step is committing to what you will do. **Understanding what you can do, and understanding**

what you want to do, and committing to what you will do are completely different thoughts and attitudes.

The *Get Attitude Playbook* is something that, if committed to, will give you answers, reveal strengths and weaknesses and provide you with the map to get you from what you can do, to understanding what you want to do to actually committing and doing it.

Attitude Transformation Opportunity- Go to your *Get Attitude Playbook* and write your answer this question.

Are you actively engaged and committed to what you will do when it comes to a challenge or attitude in your life?

Go ahead...write down one thing that you are committed to doing and do it!

Part Four

The Attitude of Effort

GOALS

Continue your Attitude transformation by:

- Identifying the Eight Areas of Voluntary Effort
- Living the Ten Attributes of Effort

Chapter 13

The Secret is Effort

Effort is defined as the physical or mental energy needed to do something. As you're going through your deals after deals after deals, you're going, "Man, I'm feeling worn. I'm feeling tired. I don't feel like I can deliver. I don't have that mental or physical energy that I need." It happens. Fatigue happens to us all. When I get tired, I start thinking, "Man, what's my purpose here? Why am I doing this?" Your purpose will pull you through. STOP and think "what is my purpose" that is the fuel of your effort.

Here's the thing, the opposite of that energy is stress. We become worn down. Our mental and our physical energy is done. I know that you may have a lot going on and are to capacity. You're full.

There's one way out of stress, and it's a shot. It's called an effort shot. Effort is the antidote to stress. If you are feeling stressed, one very simple thing is to get out and move. Get out and exercise. When stress is occurring, you need to fight that with effort. Don't cave, don't waver, don't not believe, don't bitch at a co-worker, don't be complaining. Let's just get on that horse, and ride that effort right through our challenges, because effort will get you through. Sometimes, you do need to kick your own ass.

Ten seconds of effort could change it all. I'm not here to tell you that you've got to put in more effort. I'm here to open your mind, to get you thinking and to help you analyze where you're putting that effort and have effective it is. **"Am I putting the effort in all the areas of my life that I need to?"**

Oftentimes, we focus our effort in the wrong areas. We don't put our effort into pursuing our dreams. We are afraid that the effort we put into our dreams won't amount to anything. Break free of that mentality. I love this Commencement speech by Jim Carrey that clearly communicates the importance of putting effort into what you love:

You can spend your whole life imagining ghosts, worrying about the pathway to the future, but all that will ever be is what's happening here, and the decisions we make in this moment, which are based in either love or fear. So many of us choose our path out of fear disguised as practicality. What we really want seems impossibly out of reach and ridiculous to expect, so we never dare to ask the universe for it.

- I'm saying, I'm the proof that you can ask the universe for it. My father could have been a great comedian, but he didn't believe that that was possible for him, and he made a conservative choice. Instead, he got a safe job as an accountant. When I was 12 years old, he was let go from that safe job, and our family had to do whatever we could to survive.
- I learned many great lessons from my father, not the least of which was that you can fail at what you don't want, so you'd might as well take a chance on doing what you love.

All right. Are you doing what you love? You can fail at what you don't want, so why not take the risk and put effort into your passions? The other big "a-ha" in that was that people take the path of least resistance. We don't take the harder path. The harder path is known as effort. Here's what I got from his speech. The biggest gamble in life is your effort. Your effort's the biggest gamble in life that you're taking. You know what? Some bet more than others, and my guess is that those who are on the top of their industry are betting a little bit more on their effort than you're betting on yours.

My goal is to be the greatest speaker in America. I can tell you, I know who I'm gunning for, and I'm putting in the effort, and I'm planting the seeds, and it will happen. I believe that. Who are you gunning for in your marketplace? Healthy competition is great. How much are you willing to gamble?

Chances are, your 1099 income is a reflection of your willingness to gamble on your effort. How many times do you do the bare minimum for a project? Maybe if you put in a couple more minutes of effort into that project, it could turn into something amazing.

Effort is not your enemy.

I know that there are two different types of effort. I want to first focus on life's effort, and what is called "forced effort." We all have forced effort, and I'm going to introduce you to several different scenarios.

Number one, our troops, right? Are you a member of the military, or do you know somebody who is? I know you fight that effort every day. I've started with the military, because there are no greater heroes in my life than those who put their lives on the line for us. There's no greater example of effort. As I grew up and overcame all my challenges, I always thought of myself as a Marine, or as an Army guy. That's the quintessential example of effort.

If you've ever had a sick child, where you don't know if they're going to win or if they're going to lose, you're dealing with forced effort. NFL player Devon Still is the strongest man you'll ever meet, but his little girl has cancer. If you've ever had a sick child, that takes effort. It's effort that you carry around with you as caregivers.

If you have a friend or a parent who's in a wheelchair or restricted, that can't move their limbs, that's effort. I can't tell you about forced effort. I know, this is the effort you're putting forth every day. If you have a parent or someone you care about who has Alzheimer's; you're dealing with that right now; that's forced effort.

Have you ever been cared for? Are you a person that somebody's had to care for? That's effort. One of the hardest things in life to deal with, especially if you are fiercely independent, is to allow yourself to be cared for.

That's tough. Joe Flitcraft was an all-state football player, almost graduated. After the football season, he was sledding, and he broke his neck; he is a now quadriplegic. Do you know somebody that broke his neck in an accident, that had to be cared for? My favorite story is when I asked, "Joe, how long do those wheelchairs go for?" He said, "Seven miles." I said, "How'd you know that?" The great thing about Joe, and the great thing about all these people, is that they don't let the effort they're putting forth define them. Joe's been a defensive football coach, defensive line coach, for the past 8 years. I was with Joe getting an award, and his spirit endures.

Addiction. The number one problem we're having in America with our youth is heroin addiction. It is bad, and it's cheap, and it's accessible. If you're a parent or a friend, or if your parents were drunks or whatever, if you've been affected by addiction, I can't talk to you about effort, because you're living with it every day. That loneliness, that lonely feeling; whether you're related to somebody with the addiction or not, or if you're food addicted, or whatever it is. Battling that addiction takes effort.

How about this? Have you ever been bullied? Trust me, I was bullied. I was the youngest of 4 boys; ass kicked regularly. It was like, "Good morning, it's 8 o'clock, it's ass-kicking time." If you've ever been faced by a bully at at school, home, or even work, it takes effort to face that. Have you ever been the one that people are talking behind your back and saying, "She can't do it. She can't do it," or being made fun of, or "We work at a better company"? I don't know, but if you've been a victim of bullying, you get it.

If you can't relate to any of the above scenarios, you should feel very fortunate. Everyone is doing something to save lives and to help people. You are a part of something bigger than you. I'm not here to preach about forced effort, the effort life demands from us day in and day out. I know a lot of you are struggling with one of these things, or many more. The bottom line is, everybody's trying to find a secret to making it work.

In business everyone is trying to find the magic bullet to work less and make more.

Sometime people turn to solutions presented in books, such as *Work the System, The Simple Mechanics of Making More and Working Less, Work Less and Make More, Do Less Work and Make More Money*. Guess what? BS. It doesn't work. The only people making money off of working less, are people selling books about working less, right? It doesn't happen. Everybody's looking for the secret.

The Secret is Effort!

I want to talk about the Eight Areas of "Voluntary Effort." Voluntary effort is the extra effort you put into your life, relationships, and work. You volunteer to put the extra effort into everything you do. We have this forced effort placed upon ourselves. Life puts us in stressful and overwhelming scenarios like the ones above, but then we become entrepreneurial when we have "voluntary effort." We're like, "I can do this. I'm going to dominate my market." I want you to grade yourself, on a scale of 1 to 10, in these 8 areas of voluntary effort.

Area number 1: Leadership - You don't have to be a manager to lead. Your team could be associated vendors of your business, referral partners, and subordinates. Whoever they are, they should be your best friends. Everybody's leading a team. One of the guys I loved to study for leadership was General Schwarzkopf. What do you think General Schwarzkopf said the number one key identifier in leadership is? Great leaders tell the TRUTH. That's what Schwarzkopf said. You tell the truth to yourself. You tell it to your troops, and you tell it to each other. The reason why is this; most people lie to themselves; not you, of course.

There are people around you, surrounding you, who lie to themselves. Man, it's the ability to tell the truth as a leader that will help you grow and help you triple your business.

I also heard a fantastic quote about leadership from John Addison CEO of Primerica he stated, "Leadership is not a position it's a disposition." I believe this to be true, what is your disposition when you step up to lead? Leadership mostly occurs when there is an opportunity to fill a void and step up, leadership is just not necessarily given.

Area number 2: Growing a Business - The decision to start a business is one thing, the decision to grow a business is quite different. Growing a business involves some painful and tough decisions. Decisions like personal collateralization, increased risk, increased overhead, and increased personal investment of time and effort. Conflicts also grow as you decide to grow a business: conflict with partners, conflicts on decision making, conflicts on vision of the future. We call all the above growing pains. Are you putting forth the effort to grow? On a scale of 1 to 10, how much growing pains are you ready to experience? I don't know what's healthy or what's not healthy. Some people say 3, some people say 10, but you need to experience some level of pain as you push yourself and your business to improve; that's effort. Wanting to grow, having the vision to grow, committing to grow, that takes effort.

Area number 3: Competing - Play like you are in first...train like you are in second!

In any competition, there is an underdog and a favorite. The key to dominating competition is by being able to channel both energies. This saying has stuck with me daily, I hope it sticks with you.

When you consider being the favorite, one must realize that confidence, experience and talent are three ingredients to win. In terms of pressure to win, some believe the favorite actually has more pressure on them. I believe they only do because they haven't trained like they were in second. If you are better, you are better; there is no pressure. This would be like a Division 3 football team playing the likes of a National contending Division 1 team. Simply put, they are going to lose. No matter what they believe, how they adjust or what they do. They simply are not better. Does it happen on the rare occasion that a big underdog upsets the favorite? Yes, but very rarely. When they do, those losses can be attributed to that favorite not training like number 2.

However, where this gets interesting is when there is a slight favorite in the competition. Where number 2 is on their heels. Whether it is in sports or in sales or productivity, if you are not number 1, if you train like a beast, you can get there, but without the confidence or belief (if you have never risen to number 1), it is still tough to capture. Being number 1, or the best, allows you to perform with extreme confidence, belief and skill; if you are not number 1, you need to channel these three components into your game plan.

Competition is an interesting dynamic. How competitive are you? How much do you expose yourself to competition? If you tend to shy away from competition, I have no problem with that. Your life may be a lot less hectic and stressful for sure. However, lack of competition creates its own stress in the form of lack of growth, knowledge and overall complacency with life. I've seen people in this state, and it ain't pretty.

If you are not playing like you are number 1, if you are not training like you are number 2, what are you doing? If you are truly happy, I say continue what you are doing. If you are not, I say stir up a little competition in your life. Being judged is one thing…being judged by really great people is another. It can be FUN, if you have the right ATTITUDE!

We've been very fortunate. I've been fortunate to coach for a high school football team who possesses 13 state championships. We never limit ourselves with only scouting. We know what they do, but we are about reaching our full potential with practice and repetition. I compete every day. God, I love to compete. I get up and I say, "Who am I going to go compete today?" I'm going to go compete, period. It is just how I am made.

This quote was said to me, "Glenn, be open to being challenged by great people." That has been great advice! Put yourself in a position to do that.

Coach John Wooden said, "Just worry about yourself." While competition is essential, focusing on the competition all the time is not beneficial. Focusing on your improvement and development is more beneficial to you and those who surround you.

When you are constantly competing, you can fall in the trap of becoming obsessed with what you opponent or your peer is doing. Yes, this was me. Always looking at the sales boards. Monitoring what the people better than me were doing. I still have trouble with this.

I was taught that I was a creature who craved significance in his life more than any other emotional need.

Here are the problems with focusing on what others are doing:

1. You do not congratulate, appreciate or encourage others achievements.
2. You will always lose because there is someone always better thus setting yourself up for disappointment over and over again.
3. You cannot operate at your highest level because you are distracted by others achievements.
4. This means less reps, less reading, less specialization, less focus.
5. You create false expectations, both good and bad, of your opponent and or competitor.
6. You can over-estimate or under-estimate their ability and execution.
7. You can over analyze and become paralyzed.

Whatever you are doing in life, I can assure you there are thousands of people doing the same thing. You do not have time to digest all their information. It may be wrong, it may not be as good as yours, and **if you keep swallowing what others do, you will have no hunger to create for yourself.**

There are tens of thousands of personal development gurus out there. I had to shut them off, do my thing and now I've written this book. No longer do I say, "I can never be as good as them." I just need to be the best me possible for me!

"If you coach, you are going to get out coached." **The most important person you coach is you!** Good Luck! This book is helping you become your best coach. **You are your ultimate competition. Get Attitude and get after yourself!**

AREA number 4: Adjusting - The ability to make adjustments at halftime is essential in the game of football (or any sport), at work, and in life!

I was a position coach in football for roughly 25 years. I played the game since I was in Kindergarten. The game taught me a lot, the people in the game taught me more. This is for all the players, coaches, managers, medical staff, fans, everyone associated with the teams I was involved in. We don't take time daily to have a halftime. Most of us run through a day, beginning to end, without stopping and pausing to analyze what we are doing, how we are approaching and how we are executing in the day. We also do not take the time to see how our competitors (which could be time, another salesperson, another leader, etc.) are approaching us, executing their strategy, and affecting what we do. In my book, everyday is game day. Forces outside of you are trying to capture your mind, compete for your soul and win over your attitude. Take the time at some point in the day to STOP even for just five minutes and analyze who is doing what to your game plan and execution of your day, week, or month.

Just think, if you really took the time to lay your day out like a "game plan," execute that game plan, then at 12 noon say, "It is halftime, what do we need to adjust?"

With almost certainty, I can tell you at halftime, the number 1 thing most people need to adjust is their attitude!

Days can start wrong; you wake up late, there's no coffee in the cupboard, you run out of gas on the way to work, your cell phone breaks, you flat tire pulling in to your early appointment, you get denied three times on three consecutive sales calls... Yea, that will influence your attitude, if you attitude is weak. However, now take the time to get in your "locker room", plan out the second half, visualize victories, and always believe that the next play is going to turn out better than the last. We used to ask our players, "What is the most important play of a football game?" Answer: The next play! I am suggesting that you ask yourself, "What is the most important hour in your day?" You got it...the next hour! One of my mentors, Michael M. Bill, actually drilled this philosophy down to this, "Am I doing the most productive thing I can do every minute of the day?" Do you? If you do or if you start, you will see enormous gains in productivity and success. Just think what your life would be like if you can conceptualize every minute being more valuable than the last?

When I was coaching football, most of the time when we won, and we won a lot, it was because of our half time adjustments. I think it's smart for you as a person to have a half time in a day, and to sit down and say, "How did my morning go, and what do I need to adjust?" How many people have wasted a morning before? How bout a day, a week, a month? You get the picture, not taking the time to assess where you are will haunt you later in life. I congratulate you for undertaking this book and playbook because reading it and doing the exercises are exactly what this anecdote is all about.

I've also been doing this practice in my business. Every Wednesday, we have a half time; I love half time. If you don't have a halftime in your day, I say get one and see if your productivity increase and your stress decreases. If you do not believe you are being challenged in one way or another every hour of everyday, you are wrong. You are, you just don't know it; your attitude won't let you believe it, so take a halftime break to check yourself and your game plan.

Every day, have a half time. Every week, have a half time. Every month, half time, and adjust. Let's look at what's going on. Let's be aware of what's happening. Let's ask ourselves, "What do we need to stop doing? What do we need to start doing? What do we need to continue doing?" Adjusting; on a scale of 1 to 10, what's my effort when it comes to making adjustments? Or, do you say, "Screw it, I'm not changing. I'm not adjusting." That would be a 1. If you're a guy that loves to plot and scheme and adjust, then you'd be a 10. I want you to score yourself on this area.

Area number 5: Decisiveness - Decisions, especially the hard ones, take effort. Hard decisions take effort. Are you a person that makes hard, tough decisions? 1 to 10, where are you? It takes effort to make a choice. It doesn't take any effort just to not decide. It's very simple. "We'll just keep going. We won't adjust, we won't decide, and then we're going to go broke." As Zig Ziglar said, "Timid salesmen have skinny kids." You've got to make some decisions. You can't be afraid to make the difficult choices in life.

The thing that General Schwarzkopf taught me when I heard him speak was that when he looks for leaders, he looks for people who are quick decision makers. When I was selling real estate, I was 20 years old. I was kicking everybody's butt, selling, selling, and this guy comes up to me. The guy is like, "You had a typo on your flyer. You're really going to send that flyer out?" I said, "Yes, I'm sending the flyer out. I don't care. I'm decisive."

He took a week to make his flyer perfect. My flyers went out, and I had 3 listings before he sent anything out. Hello; that's called decisiveness. I'm not saying be sloppy, but mistakes happen. Here's the thing about decisiveness; the biggest benefit is that I'm going to know if I'm wrong quicker. By not making decisions, I'm not going to know if I'm wrong or not. Not knowing if I am wrong could cost me in my relationships, my pocketbook and my attitude. I put forth the effort, and I became more decisive.

Area number 6: Committing - How committed are you to your business? Are you on a team? Are there people on your team that are not as committed as you? This is a great thing to share with the people you're working with. I'm not afraid to tell people, "You are not committed to what we are doing." Committed people in relationships do not fear tough honest talk. Pat Riley said, "It's very simple, and you're either in or you're out." A great example of commitment is examining how hard your colleague is willing to challenge and pull you; passive people are not committed, engaged people will put you through the ringer to uplift your results.

We created a shirt for our team it said on the back, "Commitment: you've either got it or you don't." The reality is there's no halfway. You either have it, or you don't. There are people who you're getting ready to work with or speak to, or there's people on your team in your office that are not committed. You need to assess the people around you and their commitment level to you, your cause or your business, and determine if they are either committed or not. If not, you need to adjust your relationship. Part of the reason people are not committed is because you may not have a clear vision for them. Part of the reason people aren't committed is they don't know exactly what is going on. If you are a leader, it's important that you're very clear, and that you can get them to commit to a clear goal.

AREA number 7: Attitude - Well this book is about attitude, so the need for an explanation here is not needed. The question is on a scale of 1 to 10, how much are you working on your attitude? How much will you continue to work on your attitude after you read this book? Do you work on your attitude every day? Do you wake up with a good attitude? Attitude is simply the way you dedicate yourself to the way you think. How are you dedicating yourself to the way you think?

AREA number 8: Differentiation - How much of an effort are you making to be different in your marketplace from your competitors? What does that mean in your approach? One thing I've asked over the past few years is how many approaches do you have for a customer or potential customer? Is it this? "Hi, you wouldn't want to give me any business, would you?" or this, "Hey, I already know that you have a relationship with another rep but..." Right, that's not a good approach.

How different is your approach? How many different approaches to clients do you have? I have a system for getting inside the heart and mind of a client. Number 1 is target. I want you to think that you are all now head coaches, and what's the first thing you need as a head coach to have a winning team?

Players, and talent. There are 5 players in each of your marketplaces right now that you need to own. I want you to say, "I am the head coach of the basketball team. I am looking for 5 players." That's called targeting. Target those 5. Then, I want you to engage them, then recruit them, and then say, "You're my starting 5." I'm only asking for 5, but if you creatively approach them, you will get them. Most of all, if you put forth the effort, you will.

Effort is sometimes defined as an attempt to do something that is difficult or that involves hard work. One of my favorite sayings is by William Barclay, "There are two great days in a person's life - the day we are born and the day we discover why." Everybody's like, "Find your why, find your why." Look; your why will find you. Don't push it too far, but you put in the effort. Effort occurs when you really, really believe in something.

> **I ask that you believe in yourself more than anybody else. If you believe in yourself and what you can do, the effort will be there.**

Attitude Transformation Opportunity - Go to your *Get Attitude Playbook* and write down the scores that you gave yourself in all eight areas of voluntary effort.

- In Leadership, I gave myself a score of ____ because…
- In Growing a Business, I gave myself a score of ____ because…
- In Competing, I gave myself a score of ____ because…
- In Adjusting, I gave myself a score of ____ because…
- In Decisiveness, I gave myself a score of ____ because…
- In Committing, I gave myself a score of ____ because…
- In Attitude, I gave myself a score of ____ because…
- In Differentiation, I gave myself a score of ____ because…
- What area is your best?
- What area of effort do you need to focus on improving?

Chapter 14

Ten Attributes of Effort

When you have an Amazing Attitude, and you're putting in extra effort, there is a positive snowball effect. Along with effort comes these attributes. Learn about these attributes and rate yourself on a scale of 1-10.

The Number 1 Attribute of Effort is Focus. It takes effort to stay focused. Focus is an attribute of effort that is everything. Laser focus; on a scale of 1 to 10, how focused are you on your business? How focused are you on your team? How focused are you on your effort? It's easy to not be focused. Focus is an attribute of effort, and I know that the most focused business person usually wins, not the one that's out chasing everything; consistent focus, every day. Next is personal accountability. Am I personally accountable to myself? Ray Lewis has a quote, "Wins and losses come a dime a dozen, but effort, nobody can judge effort." Effort is between you and you. Effort ain't got nothing to do with nobody else.

We all like to judge and look at everybody else's effort, but the bottom line is, you need to look inside and say, "Have I really put forth the effort in all these different areas that I need to focus on?" Do you have the effort to compete against yourself? I mentioned voluntary effort and competition. The biggest competition you have is you, right? Do you have the effort it takes to compete against yourself; to get in early, to stay late?

Attribute Number 2 is Enthusiasm. If you increase your enthusiasm, people will become attracted to you, and it becomes contagious. Nobody wants to do business with someone who is unenthusiastic, right? Ralph Waldo Emerson wisely said, "Enthusiasm is the mother of effort and without it nothing great was ever achieved." If you have no enthusiasm, you will not be able to create effort. It will dwindle your energy, and without it, nothing great was ever achieved.

Attribute Number 3 is Perseverance. As Winston Churchill said, "Continuous effort- not strength or intelligence, is the key to unlocking our potential." He was pretty smart, he knew some stuff. It's continuous effort. I like to call it follow-through. How good's your follow-through? How good's your follow-up? Are you missing any opportunities? Have you missed any opportunities lately?

When you shoot the ball and you don't follow through, what happens? You fall short, clink. How's your follow-through, on a scale of 1 to 10? How's your follow-up?

Attribute Number 4 is Hard Work. Vince Lombardi said it best, "The harder I work, the harder it is to surrender." Here's the point; there's a lot of people that make it easy to surrender. They just quit. Why? Because they don't put in the hard work. They don't put in the effort. The biggest gamble that you take is the effort, and if you put in low effort, you're not gambling a lot, so what? It's easy to walk away.

I don't know whatever challenge is in front of you for your business, but the harder you work at it, the harder it's going to be for you to say, "No, I give up. I'm turning back." For example, if have a goal to create a billion dollar business (that's a goal!), it's going to take a lot of hard work, and if you're not going to put your all into achieving your goal, it's going to be easy to just say, "We're not doing it."

Attribute Number 5 is Pain Tolerance. I was on the treadmill today. I try to run a 5K each week to make sure my energy level is up. About mile number 1.75, I started getting a chest pain. I'm like, "Crap, my chest is hurting. Honey, don't worry, I'm OK." It hurt, and I just kept going, because I have pretty high pain tolerance. I'm like, I just didn't feel my best when I didn't run a 5K before. So, I ran through it. You know what? About 2.5 miles, that pain just subsided, and I'm glad I kept going. Hopefully, you are, too.

I love this quote that my brother shared with me from the Ranger Indoctrination Speech. "Humans are comfort seekers…it's the individual who does not seek comfort who is extraordinary." Are you a comfort seeker, or are you ready to go out and make things happen? Are you willing to have pain tolerance? That's coming from the Rangers, the people that I know we hold up on a pedestal, our military. They're extraordinary people because they're not comfort seekers.

My guess is for you to grow your business and become as successful as you want, you're going to have to have some pain tolerance. **Are you willing to put yourself in a state of discomfort to achieve your goals?**

Attribute Number 6 is Independent Desire. When it is all said and done, many of us want someone else to support our dreams more than we do. We want to blame it on Jake, or we want to blame it on management, or we want to blame the mailman… Look, it's your dream. It's your independent desire to do what you want to do. Nobody else matters. If you've got that independent desire to make it, nobody can take that away from you.

Attribute Number 7 is the Willingness to make Small Changes, Daily. Just small changes take effort. Just imagine, if you woke up differently, the effort to think a little differently, the effort to modify how you act at times, how you treat others, or just to smile, right? Just small little changes; one small change every single day, you can recreate yourself, but it takes effort.

Attribute Number 8 is Resourcefulness. Your resources aren't the problem. Your resourcefulness is the problem. Three keys to resourcefulness: how creative are you, how determined are you, and how caring are you? You want to create resourcefulness, creativity, determination and caring. Steve Job's greatest story on resourcefulness is when Apple's getting smoked, and they're going, "How do we compete?" What did he do? He didn't have the money, he didn't have the research, so what did he do? He changed the colors, and he made them colorful. That's resourcefulness. It didn't cost him any more money, but he was creative, he was determined, and he cared. He cared about his customers, and many of them were women. He realized, "Gals aren't buying enough of these. Let's color them up," and then all of a sudden, boom, they went crazy. Great story.

Attribute Number 9 is Confidence. It takes effort to be confident. Fake it until you make it. I don't care who you are or where you're from, I don't want to do business with someone who is not confident. A customer asks, "Do you think we can get the loan done?" You mumble, "Well, uh, I don't know." That's a killer, man. The customer will be saying, "OK, I don't think I'm going to be using you."

The difference between confidence and arrogance is likability. I don't know how likeable you are. A lot of us think we're more likable than we really are. We tend to overestimate our likability. I always ask people, "On a scale of 1 to 10, how likeable are you?"

They're like, "8." I'm like, "Cut it in half, there you are. That's about what it is." Pay attention to the way others respond to you. Make sure your confidence is connected to a positive attitude. You want to draw people in, not push them away with your arrogance.

Attribute Number 10 is Having Core Values. Number 10 is what speaks to me the most. Your core values are beautiful, and I love your core values. I have mine in my office. Humility is first. When it comes to effort, we are all drivers. We're all trying to do a billion things. We're all trying to double. We all want more. Make sure to remember your core values.

One core value is to stay family-focused. My fourth child's leaving. We're empty nesters, whew, really excited! Yet, when it was all said and done, I looked back over my 27-year career, and man, sometimes I didn't make the effort for my family. When you're busy building, and creating, and competing, and having effort, and doing all this stuff, it is very easy to leave behind and take for granted the people that love you the most. My plea to you is that as you're becoming amazing, and as you're growing your business, and as you're delivering effort, that you always stay family-focused, and give the effort to your family that they desire and deserve.

Attitude Transformation Opportunity - Core values are guiding principles that dictate behavior and action. Take out your *Get Attitude Playbook* and write down your top ten core values.

As we come to the end of *The ABC's of Attitude*, I'd like to share TEN ATTITUDE BOOSTERS that are on the back of my business cards. I treat these like they are the Ten Commandments of Attitude.

I have been asked on numerous occasions what a person can do daily to snap them into a positive attitude. I have created these Attitude Boosters as a daily shot for positive attitude. Live them, share them, and you won't be able to help yourself from being happy, positive and fulfilled.

1. **Be Nice**
2. **Have a Big Goal**
3. **Have a YES! Attitude**
4. **Do More than You Are Paid For**
5. **Have a Mentor, Copy Them**
6. **Control Your Emotions**
7. **Grow or Die**
8. **Love Adversity**
9. **Eat Right and Exercise**
10. **Be a Part of Something Bigger than Yourself**

I know an attitude transformation can seem overwhelming; however, if you follow these ten Attitude Boosters daily, you will find yourself possessing an attitude which attracts others and creates a contagious energy around your spirit. No matter where you are in the Get Attitude process, start each day by reviewing and embracing these Boosters and you'll start each day with an Amazing Attitude!

Attitude Transformation Opportunity - By reading *The ABC's of Attitude* and completing the *Get Attitude Playbook*, you have given yourself the tools you need to have an Amazing Attitude. Go to your *Get Attitude Playbook,* reflect on your journey, and write down your answer to these last questions.

- What are the three biggest attitude adjustments I have made throughout this process?
- Which Attitude Booster am I strongest at, and which one requires the most improvement of me?
- Now ask you spouse, partner or close friend the same question above on what they would say is your greatest strength and weakness when it comes to the Attitude Boosters.

CONCLUSION

"Look on every exit as being an
entrance somewhere else."
-Tom Stoppard,
Rosencrantz and Guildenstern Are Dead

Well congratulations, you've completed the book! I hope you took
the time to complete the Playbook as well. If you are anything like
me you probably just read through this first and will tackle the
Playbook at a later date. For those of you who actually completed
the whole process, I want to give you special kudos and admiration
because this process can be a bit grueling, eye opening, and
uncomfortable.

I realize there are positions of thought in this book that you may
have disagreed with, and that is great. I hope this book, for the
most part, made you think and feel about how your Attitude was
shaped in the past, how it was influenced by others, and how
much ownership you are taking of it now. The fact you got to the
end tells me you own your attitude, and the great thing is no one
can ever take that from you.

I believe every attitude on this earth is worth exploring,
developing and embracing. Every attitude I run into teaches me as
much as I hope I taught you. I want you to realize I am a facilitator

of thoughts and feelings. I am not here, nor did I write this book, to judge you, only to free you from self limiting thoughts you may be putting on others and, most importantly, yourself. I hope and pray at some point in your journey through this book you had an awakening and created a new way of thought and new feelings about how you think. I hope that this new way affects you profoundly and allows you to show up to others and yourself as a shining light that is positive, deep, and motivating. I hope that when you meet others they feel more attracted to you as you do them. My guess is you are more attractive than you think you are, but conversely so are those you come across in life.

Changing the world one attitude at a time is a gift I hope you share with me. I hope you can see it happening all around you. I hope you can feel it in your life and in every relationship you are currently in and in every relationship you set out to embark on. The attitude you have created in this book should excite you, motivate you and create a vitality in your life that is both attractive and contagious to you and everyone you meet.

I do not know what is in that Playbook of yours, but I can assure you that if you look at it everyday, it will change your life. You don't need to feel the pressure and always be looking for instant change, but witness the evolution of your life as your attitude evolves. This is a daily practice, a dedication to a better way of life. Positive attitude, and the work you do for it, will create harmony that you've never felt, encouragement like you've never given, and results like you've never realized. I would love you to send me an email and share with me your biggest, wildest goal that you wrote down for yourself or share with me the most profound effect this book had on your thinking or feeling. I hope that you will soon become a student at the University of Attitude by signing up for our webinars and private courses and seminars. Most of all, I hope you share this book with someone you love who is suffering from a negative attitude, someone whose focus is in a place of despair and desperation. Perhaps the greatest feeling you will ever enjoy is bringing, or helping to bring, someone out of their way of negative thinking and negative lifestyle. Trust me, this is not easy, nor will they even want to listen at all to you, but to simply purchase this book and hand it to them with a hug may be all it takes.

If you are interested in becoming a professor at the University of Attitude and become an influencer of Attitude in your community, please contact us at influencer@universityofattitude.com and we will engage you on a process of personal transformation and achievement that you have never experienced.

Come join us, ride the wave of attitude, and
change the world one attitude at a time.
You are worth it and the ones you love are too!

RESOURCES

Here are a few resources that have inspired me, and have helped others develop their Amazing Attitudes! All of thee fantastic programs, books, and mentors that have been mentioned or quoted in *The ABC's of Attitude* are listed here. I've even included some of my favorites that aren't in the book. Take some time to explore, read, or purchase these resources while continuing your attitude transformation! Remember, G is for Grow or Die!

Websites:

- University of Attitude: Get Attitude! - You've learned the ABC's of Attitude, but that is just the start! Check out the University of Attitude and learn about training, workshops, and events at http://UniversityofAttitude.com
- Coach Wooden - Learn more about this legendary coach and teacher. Check out the Memory Wall, Favorite Maxims, and Coach's Bookstore for tons of Amazing Attitude inspiration! http://www.coachwooden.com/

Books, Programs, & Videos:

- *Live Full Die Empty* by Les Brown - Watch part of this great motivational speech about becoming whoever you want to be. https://youtu.be/dcGj6mfzDuw

- *Chicken Soup for the Soul* by Jack Canfield and Mark Victor Hansen - "The classic book that inspired millions! You will find hope and inspiration in these 101 heartwarming stories about counting your blessings, thinking positive, and overcoming challenges."
- *How to Win Friends and Influence People* by Dale Carnegie - "A timeless bestseller, packed with rock-solid advice that has carried thousands of now famous people up the ladder of success in their business and personal lives."
- Jim Carrey's Commencement Speech - An inspiring speech about pursuing your goals. Check out the entire speech here https://youtu.be/V80-gPkpH6M
- *Quiet Strength: The Principles, Practices, and Priorities of a Winning Life* by Tony Dungy - "Coach Dungy tells the story of a life lived for God and family—and challenges us all to redefine our ideas of what it means to succeed."
- *Little Gold Book of Yes! Attitude, Little Red Book of Selling,* and *Social Boom* by Jeffrey Gitomer - "You say you weren't born with a YES! attitude? No problem! Jeffrey Gitomer will give you all the tools you need to build one. He's brought those lessons together in the *Little Gold Book of YES! Attitude* and it will change your life!"
- *The Compound Effect* and *Roller Coaster Entrepreneur* by Darren Hardy - "A distillation of the fundamental principles that have guided the most phenomenal achievements in business, relationships, and beyond."
- *Think and Grow Rich* by Napoleon Hill - "Inspired by Andrew Carnegie's magic formula for success, this book will teach you the secrets that will bring you a fortune."
- *The Official Guide to Success* by Tom Hopkins - "Overcome emotional handicaps and break free from the past through Tom's variety of topics."

- *The Greatest Salesmen in the World* by Og Mandino - "What you are today is not important…for in this runaway bestseller you will learn how to change your life by applying the secrets you are about to discover in the ancient scrolls."

- *Become a Better You* by Joel Olsteen - "Not only can you live happily every day, you must discover the potential within yourself and learn how to use it to live better, and to help others better themselves as well."

- *Awaken the Giant Within* by Anthony Robbins - Wake up and take control of your life! The nation's leader in the science of peak performance shows you his most effective strategies and techniques for mastering your emotions, your body, your relationships, your finances, and your life.

- *Challenge to Succeed* by Jim Rohn - "The legendary Jim Rohn's most popular seminar presentation. Discover five inspirational topics that guide the participant through self-evaluation and commitment."

- The Big Book of Alcoholics Anonymous by Dr. Bob Smith and Bill Wilson - "A basic text, describing how to recover from alcoholism written by the founders of Alcoholics Anonymous."

- *Think Big and Kick Ass in Business and Life* by Donald Trump - "For the first time ever, you too can learn Trump's secrets to thinking BIG and kicking ass!"

- *Pushing Up People: The Secret Behind One of the Most Exciting Success Stories in America* by Art Williams - "Williams teaches and shares the breathtaking saga of "average-ordinary" people who teamed up to do the impossible."

- *See You at the Top* by Zig Ziglar - "This inspirational volume teaches the value of a healthy self-image and how to build that image. It clarifies why goals are important, teaches you how to set them, and motivates you to reach them."

Fitness Programs: Remember, E stands for Effort, Enthusiasm, Energy, Eat Right & **Exercise**

- Jack LaLanne - "The Godfather of Fitness" Revolutionized the way we think about health and exercise. No matter what your age is or what your fitness goals are, you'll benefit from LaLanne's philosophy. http://www.jacklalanne.com/
- Martin Rooney's Training for Warriors - A fitness program originally created for the best combat athletes. The training methods of the TFW system can benefit anyone looking to lose fat, build muscle and feel good. http://www.trainingforwarriors.com/

ABOUT THE AUTHOR

Glenn Bill is a serial entrepreneur and ravenous learner of attitude and self-improvement.

He began his career as a REALTOR and Asst. H15. Football Coach. He was aligned with extraordinary people who helped raise him to high levels of success in both arenas, and he is extremely thankful and humbled by their impact on his life, studies and attitude.

Shortly after the start of his sales career, he purchased a franchise business and, together with two partners, grew it into one of the largest franchises in the world. He continued to coach during this expansion as well as sell to his large network. Glenn's attitude and passion carried him through these very busy years, while he was juggling three careers at once!

However, his most important accomplishment and greatest source of inspiration for his attitude and passion is the fulfilling life he has created with his childhood sweetheart and wife and their four children. They are the WHY behind his drive, success and fulfillment.

After seventeen years as a Broker/Owner, Glenn sold his real estate brokerage business and began to educate, train and inspire others using the techniques, insights and effort he learned from his mentors.

He derived his content for his first two programs from the seventeen years of sales meetings he produced for his rapidly growing companies. One is primarily a real estate sales training program called *Source of Sales* (How To Sales Training for REALTORS) and the other is a program called *Stretch* (A Personal Development Program for Salespeople).

Glenn's latest endeavor is the University of Attitude. His goal: to change the world one attitude at a time.

He is the author of <u>The ABC's of ATTITUDE</u>: *Discover Your Secret Formula to Achieve Success in Your Personal and Business Life, Increase Your Emotional Intelligence and GET ATTITUDE!* He speaks nationally to audiences that thirst for increased production, profitability and morale for their team or company.

Visit <u>www.UniversityOfAttitude.com</u> to learn more about Glenn and the University of Attitude.

CPSIA information can be obtained at www.ICGtesting.com
Printed in the USA
LVOW06*1222261015

459763LV00001B/1/P